GHOSTS AND LEGENDS OF CALICO

The town of Calico, California, was granted historical status as Landmark No. 7 on May 12, 1973. In 2005, Governor Arnold Schwarzenegger designated Calico as the official Silver Rush Ghost Town of California.

GHOSTS AND LEGENDS OF CALICO

BRIAN CLUNE

WITH BOB DAVIS

HAUNTED America

Published by The History Press
Charleston, SC
www.historypress.com

First published 2020

Manufactured in the United States

ISBN 9781467146593

Library of Congress Control Number: 2020938499

DEDICATION

Growing up, I always knew I was adopted. It never really bothered me because the people who took me in loved me, took care of me, were always there for me and were my family. My mother, father and sister were always just normal to me, as any family dynamic is. I wondered every now and then if I had any biological siblings and who my biological mother and father might be, but because I grew up in a family that loved me and cared for me, it was never that important to find out. All that changed in 2018, when my wife signed me up for a DNA test, and my biological sister made contact with me. The acceptance from this family I never knew, including my biological mother, was more than I ever could have dreamed of, and the love and caring that has come from them has made me happier than I could have imagined. So, I dedicate this book to my newly found mom, Tina; my little (he'll hate that) brother, Mick; and my baby sister, Sheila. It is also dedicated to my older sister, Maureen, who I grew up with and who has always supported me and my writing, even though she tells me what to say when I'm signing a book to her.

—Brian Clune

The cross on top of the Calico Cemetery is silhouetted against King Mountain and the now-famous town name painted at its crest.

This is the town of Calico, a town that used to be.
Up among bright colored hills, above an old, dead sea.
Where the wind blows the sand in mounds, and the canyons return the echoing sounds.

—Lucy B. Lane, the longest recorded resident of Calico

CONTENTS

Unless otherwise specified, the photographs in this book were provided by the authors.

FOREWORD

While reading *Ghosts and Legends of Calico*, I was taken back to the many experiences of my own that I have had with the unseen, yet ever-present, spirits of Calico Ghost Town. Having experienced over twenty years of living in the Calico Valley and several more in the town of Calico itself, I have become eerily familiar with many of the ghosts who chose to remain as ever faithful residents in Calico after their bodies were laid to rest in the nearby cemeteries of Dagget or Calico.

I have been asked on more than one occasion if I believe in ghosts, and my answer is always the same: "Yes!" If that makes me crazy, so be it. The souls of miners and cooks, the voices of the ladies working the saloons and even Tumbleweed Harris with his burro have been spotted on occasion. They still frequent the shops that run daily in the little town, and they touch the unaware visitor from time to time. During the twenty years Jill and I owned businesses in town, we experienced the Calico spirits in both the daytime and at night.

I think you will find this book full of fun and informative retellings of the histories of the areas around Calico and of some of the haunts that happen there. Reading the history again makes me miss the old town a bit. I have since moved out of the state, but this town and the Mojave Desert stay in my thoughts. My wish is that the reader will be able to make a trip out to see the town for themselves and experience what life must have been like for those souls so long ago.

I would like to thank Brian and Bob for a job well done with this book. I hope it serves to educate and entertain many people long after I also become an old ghostly spirit in Calico!

Happy reading and enjoy Calico!

—Bill Cook,
author of *Bill Cooks Ghostly Guide to Calico Ghost Town*

ACKNOWLEDGEMENTS

We would again like to thank our acquisitions editor, Laurie Krill. Laurie, you are truly the best editor a writer could ask for. To the other wonderful editors and staff at Arcadia and The History Press, you have our deepest respect and thanks for the hard work you all do making us look our best. We would also like to thank all of the wonderful people at Calico Ghost Town for their stories, their growing friendship and their patience while we asked all of our questions. These people are saints—especially you, Kayla! Even the rangers at Calico, who have an aversion to anything ghostly, would talk and answer questions about the history and haunts of the town, and we truly appreciate their time.

We would also like to thank the Mojave River Valley Museum which allowed us to peruse their archives and use some of their historic photos of Calico. The museum's help made this book not only a tale of the town's haunts but a true telling of the important place in history Calico has had in the development of the area and California.

As always, we have to thank Terri Clune for her support and for being our initial editor (even if she does edit my Facebook posts, too!)

Last, and assuredly not least, we would like to thank Arcadia and The History Press for still having faith in us and our writing.

The town of Calico today, as seen from the lookout point on top of the Maggie Mine.

INTRODUCTION TO CALIFORNIA'S OFFICIAL SILVER TOWN

The town of Calico was a quintessential American mining camp. There, silver was discovered, prospectors came to make their fortunes, storekeepers and saloon owners followed and close on their heels came their wives, children and families. The town grew, the people toiled all day long, the women cooked, the men drank and the whole thing began anew with the coming of each dawn. When the gold and silver ran out, the people left for greener pastures, and the town slowly died.

This same scenario was repeated over and over again across the country. From the mountains of Virginia to the gold fields of California, these seekers of wealth left rotting hulks abandoned across the pristine landscape of America to slowly fade as Mother Nature reclaimed her resources. Calico, however, was different; it refused to die. This little mining camp set in the hills of the majestic Calico Mountains, with colorful rocks and soil that gave the area its name, decided it was not going to go quietly into the night. It let Mother Nature visit but would not let her take the town away. No, Calico decided that it was its destiny to stay behind, to remain in the harsh sun and biting wind of the Mojave Desert, not for itself, but for those who came behind it. It stayed behind for those who came to learn and marvel at the way things had been, those who would remember and pass along to others what they had seen and learned of who had been.

Calico has told others what it was like to dig into solid rock for hours on end in the search for life-changing metals. It explains how hard it was to stay alive when the only water available to survive had to be shipped

Old Town Calico. *Courtesy of the Mojave River Valley Museum.*

in giant barrels carried by horses and stored in the hot desert sun. It tells people what it was like to live in dug-outs hewn into the side of a stony cliff face or dug into the hard-packed earth with only a tarpaulin or pieces of cloth overhead. Calico laments the lives lost in mine accidents and those lost in the desert, the lives taken from disease run amok, which took away parents, children and grandparents, but mostly, Calico mourns for all that has been forgotten.

Calico has put on many faces. It took on the role of entertainer when it became the inspiration for a well-known amusement park, Knott's Berry Farm. It has taken up the mantle of a tourist stop for those traveling between California and the bright lights of Las Vegas. It is a county park, campground and souvenir shop. But what Calico has truly become—what it has always been deep down in its soul—is a part of living history. A part few people know but one that will open your eyes and let you see for yourself the struggles of our forefathers, the hardships, loves and losses of those that came before. Calico, the official Silver Town of California that is still alive, still struggling, still teaching. Calico Ghost Town is California history, and yes, it is also a historic town of ghosts.

Calico lives on in the barren Mojave Desert, but it is no longer alone. Those who have toiled and striven to eke out their living among the multicolored hills still linger there. The stories of those who have come before are still vibrant in their telling, but most of all, those who have lived and died in the town that is as "pretty as a girl's calico skirt" are still there, teaching us what our past was really like.

1

THE SILVER KING IS CROWNED

The first reported mining operations in the Calico area were situated near what is known today as Victorville. The discovery of gold by Judge William Clancy of Virginia City, Nevada, caused the usual influx of prospectors, fortune seekers, drunks and brawlers to the location, which Clancy named Oro Grande Mining District. As the prospectors spread out, looking for gold or other precious metals, mines and claims began popping up all over the nearby mountainsides. Then, in 1880, mine operators Robert Waterman and John Porter found a silver vein several miles east of Victorville. The two men expanded their claims and formed the Waterman Mining District. The men transported their ore to a small settlement along the Mojave River called Grapevine. As the ore shipments grew, so did the small town, and it eventually changed its name to Waterman. Today, Waterman is known as Barstow, in honor of the Santa Fe Railroad's president, William Barstow Strong.

In an odd twist of fate, the first claim near the future town of Calico was staked by a man named Lowery Silver. (The man's name has been spelled several different ways, and the spelling depends on whose writings one is looking at; for example, it can be spelled Lars or Lowery, or Silva or Silver. Most legal documents of the time have it written as Lowery Silver.) This claim led to others flocking to the area, as Silver's claim produced more and more silver ore. As successful as his claim was, the real boom came when George Yager, Tom Warden, Hues Thomas and Yager's nephew Frank Mecham teamed up to look for a ledge of red ore that Mecham's father had found in the Calico Mountains years before. The four men did not have the funds for a prolonged search of the area, so they approached San Bernardino county sheriff John King to see if he would "grubstake" them. The men knew that King had done some prospecting and figured the sheriff might help for a share in any successful claim. King readily agreed. Ellis Miller, the owner of the Grapevine Station, also decided to grubstake the endeavor, and together, these men made Mojave Desert mining history. It took the men a while to find the ledge, but once they did, they knew that they had struck a rich vein of silver and immediately began laying out claims. This claim became the now-famous Silver King Mine, which was named in honor of the man who put up the money, John Caleb King.

The group of Sliver King mines grew quickly. Colonel H.H. Markham, who was associated with the mining at Oro Grande, heard about the success at the Calico site and made a bid to lease with an option on the group of Silver King mines. Markham paid $60,000 for the lease and immediately sunk a 150-foot shaft for a known, deep vein. The ore was so rich that Markham was able to use the money he received to take up the option on the mines. With the production of the Silver King mines running so smoothly, the Waterloo Mining Company approached Markham with an offer to purchase the group. H.H. Markham sold the Sliver King for $150,000.

The Waterloo Company was a corporation based in Milwaukee and was organized by a group of lumber executives who were in the door and window sash business. As such, they had almost unlimited resources to build and run their new investment. Ore bins were built near the top of King Mountain, which was also named for John King, along with a blacksmith shop and a boardinghouse for the workers in Calico. Soon, wagons with steel-rimmed, five-foot-tall front wheels and seven-foot-tall rear wheels, pulled by twenty mule team rigs, were rolling through the main street of Calico. The wagons were headed forty miles across the dusty desert to the stamp mill at Oro Grande. Each wagon weighed 7,800 pounds when empty, but when they were loaded, they could weigh up to 45,000 pounds. The ore in the wagons fetched $110 per pound for a year after the operation began, and the twenty-mule team was an impressive sight, rolling down the street and stretching 120 feet in front of the wagon.

Eventually, larger ore bins were needed to handle the growing amount of ore that was being mined from the Silver King Mines. This could not be done at the top of King Mountain, so new ore bins were constructed along Wall Street Canyon. To aid in getting the ore down to the new bins, an ore chute was built that led from the adit (mine entrance) down to the bins. This

A twenty-mule team at Calico, circa 1885. *Courtesy of the Mojave River Valley Museum.*

chute was extremely long, steep and was built without safety rails. The winds that came down the canyons around the Silver King Chute gusted so strong that they threatened to blow the workers right off of the chute. In the words of Herman Mellen, who helped build the massive structure, "The men needed claws like a cat to keep their grip on the trestle while they worked." The men working on the chute complained to the foremen about the danger, but nothing was done about the hazard; that is, until superintendent Albert Barber was almost blown off the chute by a strong gust of wind when he went up to the top of the structure to respond to yet another complaint. Safety rails were immediately added to the rig.

As mentioned, the ore from the Silver King Mine was transported to the Oro Grande Stamp Mill, which was forty miles away. This was a costly endeavor. To ease the cost and the strain on both the men and the pack animals, the Oro Grande Company purchased the Oriental Company's mine and mill near the town of Daggett. After enlarging the mill to fifteen stamps, the wagonloads of ore from the Silver King mines began delivering their loads to Daggett. This shortened the trip considerably. The amount of ore that had been delivered each month to Oro Grande at the time the shipments ceased was worth approximately $50,000.

The price of silver had been declining for a while, and because of this, the Waterloo Mining Company was considering selling its holdings. The mines were still producing viable ore, albeit on a smaller scale than before,

The Silver King thirty-stamp mill. *Courtesy of the Mojave River Valley Museum.*

so Waterloo held off putting it up for sale. As the price of sliver continued to drop and the silver became rarer within the stone, along with the apex rights from a lawsuit, the company finally decided to shut down the operation of the Silver King Mines in Calico. They continued to operate their other holdings, but wages for their employees were put on a sliding scale that was dependent on the price of silver.

The Silver King remained dormant until 1917, when cyanide was used to extract the silver from the tailings (soil dumps left over from mine excavations). This attempt to remove the silver only had a modest success rate and was deemed more costly than it was worth. In the 1930s, the Zenda Gold Mining Company purchased the rights to the Silver King Mine along with most of the town from Lucy Lane. Even with their modern tools and know-how, the return was minimal, and the Zenda Company didn't invest too much time or money into the endeavor. Zenda was the last mining operation at the Silver King Mine. When Walter Knott approached the company with an offer to buy Calico from them, they jumped at the chance to sell, and that was the end of mining at the famous Silver King Mine.

Throughout the years that the Silver King Mine was in operation, and even with the Waterloo, Bismarck and Odessa mining operations continuing long after the Silver King was shut down, this legendary mine was the largest single money maker and ore producer that Calico ever knew.

2.
THE DESERT SPRINGS A TOWN

Calico, California, had a typical lifespan for what started out as a simple mining camp in the Mojave Desert. From 1881 until the beginning of the twentieth century, Calico was a thriving town where people lived and died, dreamed of the future and were happy—mostly. Then, as it always seemed to happen in mining communities, the ore became scarce, the price of the silver dropped, and the townsfolk left for greener pastures in other parts of California and beyond. What was not typical, however, was the impact that this tiny, out-of-the-way town had on the history of mining within California and the legacy it left behind.

Although mining in the area actually began as early as 1871, it wasn't until 1880, when the Silver King claim was found, that the boom began, and the town of Calico was born. There is some debate about the origins of the Calico name; some say it came from an early miner's comment that the hills were "as purty as a gal's calico skirt," while others think it was more likely named for the many colors of soil and stones that make up the Calico Hills. Whatever the case, the name Calico is a fitting description and name for this historic little town.

Like most mining camps, Calico started out as a rough collection of tents, lean-tos and dug-outs scattered along a semi-level area below King Mountain, spread out among the hillsides, strung out along the canyons and across the hard-packed desert landscape. Wherever a miner could find a spot near his diggings, he set up his campsite. During that first year, living in Calico was not easy. Everything the prospectors mined had to be hauled out either by foot or with pack animals, and everything they needed to live had to be packed in the same way, including the water that the miners needed to survive in the harsh desert sun. A short time after the camp was made, a harsh spring storm raged across the area and caused a destructive flood to wash through the valley floor, forcing the miners to seek higher, safer ground. The area they moved to was a strip of land on a rise that could be fairly easily leveled. They constructed a dirt road to make it easier for wagons with supplies to access the town. The area was surveyed in the summer of 1882, and by October of that year, the town of Calico was under construction.

By this time, miners were flocking to the town, looking to stake their claims and collect their fortunes. In the next three years, over three hundred claims were registered, and the entire area was divided into three separate mining districts. One district was to the northeast of the town and became known as East Calico. There were actually two areas known as East Calico; one was set aside as a residential area for miners and their families. This area was about three miles northeast of town. The other area was referred to as the East Calico Mining District and was where the Bismarck and Occidental Mines were located. Also in this area were the Birdseye and Alhambra claims. Along what would become Wall Street Canyon, the Silver

Miners and settlers in Calico would use any materials they could find to erect dwellings wherever they could near their claims.

King Mines sprang up; in this area were the Silver King, Oriental, Burning Moscow and Red Cloud Mines. To the west of the burgeoning town, the Waterloo Group set up mines. The Waterloo Mines arguably became the most famous mines to operate near the town of Calico.

As families moved to town, they brought with them everything they owned. With few buildings or homes in the newly formed town, life was a struggle at first. Margaret Olivier came to Calico in 1882 and explained:

> We had shipped a large tent with household goods and lumber, which Mr. Olivier had delivered from Waterman [Barstow] by team to Calico, and our building was the first erected on Main Street in Calico. We left on the six-horse stage for Calico. There was no lumber for the floor of the tent, and Walter was creeping, so you can imagine my problem keeping the children clean with water hauled from Fish Pond at ten cents a gallon. We lived in the rear, while the front of the tent was partitioned with canvas for rooms and the store. I baked the first bread for camp, which we sold in the store. Many early deals for mining claims were made there.

One of the first buildings to go up in the new town was the Joe Miller Store. This makes sense because, with all of the new arrivals, goods were needed to supply them. Soon to follow were the saloons, homes, stables, more shops and stores, more saloons and the Silver King Boardinghouse. Since kids were scarce in the early days of Calico, the Silver King Boardinghouse also doubled as the town's first schoolhouse. The other early buildings in Calico were, as a surveyor's map from 1882 noted, "quite a number of dugouts in the cliffs, bush shanties, and tents." These cliffside hovels were not strictly relegated to miners trying to earn a living. In 1881, the Hyena House Hotel was established. This hotel was billed as the "finest lodging in Calico," and guests arriving in town were met by a man named William Harpold and his wheelbarrow, which had a sign attached that read, "Free bus to the Hyena." Harpold would load up guests' luggage in the one-wheeled cart and deliver both to the Hyena House, which was nothing more than holes dug into the face of a rock outcropping. The holes were supported by old barrel staves, some of which were covered with burlap bags or other tattered cloth used for privacy.

As the town grew, so did the need for water. Since the town was in the hills above the Mojave Desert, water was a scarce commodity; one could say it was almost as precious as the ore the miners were digging out of the ground. Water was brought into Calico on large tank carts from wells around the dry

Another one of Calico's interesting homesteads.

lake at the foot of the hills or near the usually dry Mojave River. These carts would carry approximately two hundred gallons of water at four cents per gallon, and the shop that ordered the water would sell it to the residents and other businesses for a small profit. Being in the hot desert sun, people would store their water barrels under their porches, in overhangs or any shade available, and they would use crude desert coolers, these were suspended cans of water with small holes in the bottom that would drip onto burlap covers so that the evaporation could keep everything cool, as a way to keep their water from becoming too hot and their food spoiling too fast.

Scarcity of water was never a good thing in any town, but for a town made out of mostly wood in the desert climate, like Calico, it could and would have devastating effects. There were several restaurants in operation in the town in 1883, and they all used wood or coal oil stoves for cooking. These coal oil contraptions were notorious for erupting without warning, and that is exactly what happened in June 1883. While Cline's Restaurant was serving lunch, its stove suddenly exploded, sending flaming hot debris out in all directions. The wood walls of the establishment caught fire, igniting Ackerman's Saloon next door and the drugstore building, and it spread so rapidly that a large portion of the town was in flames before a fire brigade could be organized. Fire buckets had to be brought from the water tanks and nearby barrels, but by the time the fire was brought under control, a large portion of Calico was in ruins. In all, seventeen buildings were destroyed, including the post office and all of its contents. While there was thankfully no loss of life in the conflagration, the monetary loss was estimated to have been $25,000 dollars, a tidy sum in 1883.

After the fire, the townsfolk realized that with the water situation being what it was, something needed to be done in case there was another fire in town. To this end, when the town was being rebuilt, it was decided that every third building would be constructed out of rammed earth adobe rather than wood as a way to prevent a fire from jumping from building to building. This idea paid off with limited success; in 1887, another fire raged through Calico, destroying another large portion of the town. On September 5, 1887, while Eugenia Porter was curling her hair for a dance that evening, her son's pet goat walked by her room on the porch; when it saw its reflection in her dresser mirror, it thought it was another goat and lunged at it. The goat turned over a lit oil lamp, which immediately caught the entire room on fire. Eugenia managed to escape the room unharmed, but unfortunately, the goat was "cremated," as Eugenia put it. Eugenia never told her parents what caused the fire, and the truth didn't come out until

Now just a welcome sign marking the entrance to the town, these water wagons were life for those living in Calico in the early days.

years later, when longtime resident Lucy Lane let it slip. The fire of 1887 was just as devastating, if not more so, than the fire in 1883. Again, the post office and all of its contents were turned to ash, as were at least three lodging houses, a number of residences and the town hall. The hall was where all of the dances, wedding receptions and other events that brought the town of Calico together, were held.

Even in tragic circumstances, there were some things that happened that brought smiles to the faces of those affected by the calamity. The fire of 1887 had one of these rare occurrences. The story goes that when the house of one William H.H. LeVan, a wealthy man in town, caught fire, William's daughter Lena had to escape the burning house by going out of her upstairs bedroom window. What happened was explained by John Lane, "What confusion there was in the big fire of 1887 in Calico. When Levan's Rooming House was burning, Nannie [Lena] threw her looking glass out the window; the looking glass was broken. She carried her pillow and bedding under one arm and a tame duck under the other to safety." Another interesting anecdote of how things went awry in the confusion of adversity came from Jim Patterson. Jim told this story about what happened to him the morning after the fire.

I almost caused a fight between two women. I found a fur coat on the street as I went down to Sheridan's Restaurant, which had not burned, at the lower end of town for breakfast, and not knowing who owned the coat, gave it to Annie Johnson, who waited on tables. When she wore the coat and met Mrs. Stacy, the woman asked Annie "What are you doing with my coat?" Annie replied, "It was given to me." Mrs. Stacy tried to take the coat off of her, and I had to be called as a referee on proof of ownership; Annie retained the coat.

There were various other fires that only caused minor damage or affected only one building. The worst of these—and only because it caused the death of a popular resident—took place in 1884, when Tom Leonard's cabin caught fire and Tom was unable to escape the flames.

The last big fire in Calico came about not in the time of wooden buildings and scarce water supplies but in 2001, amid fire engines and high-pressure water hoses. This fire began in the candle and basket shop around 2:30 a.m. on Tuesday, July 24. The cause was believed to be aging electrical lines, and the fire burned down five buildings before the fire department was able to get it under control. Fortunately, no original buildings were harmed,

Even though they were built on a windy hillside, these rock structures were more comfortable than the tents and lean-tos others had to endure.

although the damage cost just over $1 million, including the restoration of five structures and their inventories. This just goes to show that, even in modern times, old wooden structures are hard to keep safe from the ravages of flame. Imagine what it was like in the 1800s.

Even with the fires, Calico was growing rapidly. By 1885, there were seventy-five businesses operating in town. As stated, many people lived in tents, hand-hewn caves or under lean-tos. These makeshift houses gave way to adobe and wood structures, and at the town's peak, there were approximately two hundred dwellings erected in Calico. Some of these homes were built into the hillsides and canyons, but they were considerably more comfortable than the hovels that some had been forced to endure.

As the town grew, a water company was organized, and a new well that was 160 feet deep was dug near the dry lake east of the old well. This water was piped in by a three-inch line that led into two large wooden tanks on top of Tank Hill, which was very near the Runover Mill, and it was fed down into Calico by gravity alone. There were no meters at this time, so a flat rate system of payment was enforced; families paid $3 to $4 a month, depending on the size of the family, single people paid $1 and couples $2. The things that weren't installed were sewage lines to the restaurants and saloon sinks. The runoff from these establishments was allowed to drain into Wall Street Canyon, where it sank into the sand. Lucy Lane addressed this by saying, "The odor was very bad, and early in December, I became ill."

Calico was fortunate to have a doctor in town. Dr. Albert Romero Rhea arrived in Calico in 1885 and started his practice immediately; Rhea also opened a drugstore in town, near his office, in order to better serve his patients' needs. Since Rhea's office adjoined his house, it was not hard for the townsfolk to find medical care if they needed it. Dr. Rhea was a stereotypical country doctor; in other words, if a patient needed medical attention, Rhea would treat what ailed them with a promise of payment at a later date. One of the reasons for this was that he received pay from the town itself as Calico's coroner, pharmacist and, in 1893, Wells Fargo Express Company agent. Dr. Rhea was also a businessman. Rhea purchased the land and water at Fish Pond and started the Minneola Land and Water Company. The company then constructed an irrigation canal for farmland in Minneola. Albert Rhea was the doctor in Calico from 1885 to 1896; he then moved his practice to the town of Daggett and, finally, to Long Beach, California. It is unclear if he left with people owing him money for his services, but an article from the 1938 *Barstow Printer* gives us an idea of the type of man Dr. Rhea was. When asked why he would spend hours saving the life of a "worthless drunk," Rhea replied, "He owes so much money I don't dare let him die." It seems clear that the doctor was a man of character.

As was common in towns throughout the American West, if there was no doctor in town, or if the doctor was out of town, the barber would administer aid. The barber, of course, could only help out in certain situations, like removing teeth that were causing severe pain or using his sharp instruments to remove bullets or perform emergency amputations. Using the barber as a medical professional was an emergency-only endeavor. If possible, waiting for the doctor to arrive back in town made one's chances of a recovery, as well as survival, much more likely. An interesting note about barbers and their highly recognizable white-and-red barber poles is how these poles came to be. Because barbers often nicked their patrons while they were shaving, cutting hair or performing a medical procedure, at the end of each day, they would hang their washed and blood-stained towels on the poles outside their doors to dry. Over time, the damp towels left indents in the pole, and the blood stained these indents, giving the appearance of a red-and-white sign that people began to associate with barbers. This was the beginning of the now-famous red, white and, sometimes, blue poles we know today. There is still an original barber pole outside the barber shop in Calico Ghost Town.

Even good doctors couldn't always win the fight against disease in the 1800s; even in the late 1800s, epidemics would rage through mining towns. These maladies were indiscriminate, striking both the poor and wealthy. Calico was no exception. In 1885, a typhoid epidemic spread through Calico, and a number of residents died from typhoid pneumonia. Then, in 1888, a diphtheria outbreak arose with much more devastating effects. In that year, much of the town became sick. Young adults and those of middle age who were fit and healthy fared well; however, the elderly who contracted the disease were at a much greater risk of complications, as were children with developing immune systems. Many children died during this epidemic; at least three of the children are buried in the Calico Cemetery with stones marked, "diphtheria." As the children passed, the school held makeshift memorials in town, across the canyon from the schoolhouse, as a way for the other kids to honor their classmates. The area where these gatherings took place is now said to be one of those places in Calico where paranormal activity is experienced.

In the late 1880s, the price of silver was declining, and with it, the mines in Calico became less valuable. They were still producing viable ore, but as the silver market paid less per ton, the mine operators paid less for labor. The borax mines were still doing well, so some of the men

Although not from Calico, the pole outside of the barber shop is an authentic, period barber's pole.

who were working the silver mines moved over to Borate and the mines there, but others left to find higher-paying jobs. Then, in 1893, President Grover Cleveland called a special session of Congress to urge it to repeal the Sherman Act. With the act repealed, silver prices fell even further. The Waterloo Mining Company closed down the Silver King Mines in 1895, and many more were quick to follow.

Calico was dying a slow death. The price of silver continued to drop, and the production of the Borax Mines were beginning to slow. There was one last hope for the town with the coming of the 1896 presidential election. Democrat hopeful Williams Jennings Bryan, a young Nebraskan, was running against Republican William McKinley. McKinley was adamant about staying on the gold standard, whereas Bryan was just as adamant about adopting the silver standard. He was so steadfast in this pursuit that his "Cross of Gold" speech that he gave at the Chicago Convention won him the nomination. Bryan's speech demanded unlimited free coinage of silver, garnering him the nickname "Silver-Tongued Nebraskan." On the day of the 1896 election, all of Calico's population stayed up in groups, almost all wearing silver bar pins that were engraved with "16 to 1" (sixteen ounces of silver to one ounce of gold), hoping that Bryan would win. When it was all over, however, McKinley won the election, and Calico could not be saved. All but two people in Calico voted for Bryan; it is said that everyone knew who the two were, but we have no clue what may have happened to those men.

With silver hitting a low value of sixty-three cents per ounce, the mines had no choice but to close down, and with the area's borax running dry, most of the people in Calico left looking for greener pastures. The school and the post office closed in 1898; then, townsfolk began moving their buildings to the towns of Daggett, Yermo and Barstow, and by 1904, the town was all but abandoned. Borax was still being mined around Borate but when these operations ceased in 1907 only the Lanes were left living in Calico.

Over the years that Calico was returning to the desert soil, Lucy and John Lane lived in Calico now and then. During that time, travelers often came to town to look around. The Lanes would always welcome them to town and play host. In 1917, a cyanide plant was built in Calico to try and recover silver from the Silver King Mine tailings, but the return was not worth the cost, and the operation didn't last long. Some of the individuals who came to Calico were early American naturalist John Muir, naturalist and author John Burroughs, Walter Knott (who stayed on briefly to work as a carpenter to help rebuild one of the mills) and *Charlie Chan* author, Earl Derr Biggers. There were also a few state and congressional senators who passed through, wanting to see the "famous" silver town.

As the automobile became in vogue, sightseeing travelers' groups came to Calico in their new cars. One of these groups, which was on a trek from Los Angeles to Death Valley, made an overnight stop near Calico. The group spent the night in Cave Springs and parked their "machines" in the Cave Springs Corral before heading out the next day for the short trip to Calico. Of course, John and Lucy Lane, the only residents still living in the town, were there to pose for pictures with the intrepid travelers. After the photos were taken, John loaned the group some carbide lamps, as they planned to explore the Silver King Mine and spend the night in Wall Street Canyon just below the town.

Unlike the automobile adventurers of the early 1900s, Wall Street Canyon is off limits to travelers today.

Sometime in the 1930s (different years have all been named, from 1932 to 1938—in Lucy Lane's book, it is said to have been 1938, as she lived there at the time), the first Old Calico Days was held in an empty field next to the Beacon Hotel and Tavern in the city of Barstow. The following year, the event was moved to the small town of Yermo. This festival was a celebration of Calico's history, mining and contributions to the state of California. The event was suspended during World War II, but it was brought back in 1947. Then, in 1966, after the town became a popular tourist stop, the festival became a permanent celebration, and it is still held every year. The jubilee features gunfights, special mine tours, crafts, games and fun things for kids to do and explore.

In 1934, Lawrence and Lucille Coke joined the Lanes in Calico and began collecting artifacts from the town's heyday, along with some of the colorful rocks and stones that were scattered over the hills of the Calico Mountains. Once the couple had a good assortment of odds and ends, they cleaned up the old A.R. Rhea Drugstore and opened up a museum and rock shop for the tourists that were arriving in town. By the time the Federal Writer's Project, a federal encyclopedia creation program that was created to provide employment for teachers, writers, historians and other educators, arrived in 1947, Lucy Lane was living in Julian, California, so

Even though the Cooks moved from Calico, Lucille was buried in the Calico Cemetery.

the researcher of the Writer's Project noted that the Cokes were the only residents. When Larry and Lucy Coke moved from Calico in 1949, the town was finally abandoned.

At its peak, from 1885 through 1886, Calico had a busy business district with a post office, schoolhouse, stables, blacksmith shop, newspaper, numerous boardinghouses and hotels, a Chinatown, a red-light district (including a mobile brothel) and twenty-two saloons but no church (the schoolhouse doubled as a place of worship). One thing that was a bit unusual for a mining town was that Calico had no bank. The population in Calico had reached a high of 3,500 people, but at the time Walter Knott purchased the town, the sign people saw as they entered Calico read, "Pop. 2."

Lucy Lane did come back to Calico, but she rented a room from a Mrs. Emma Connell, "to be close to Calico." Even though the town was then truly a ghost town, the tourists still came. By 1949, rumors had begun to surface that a man named Knott was interested in buying Calico from the Zenda Mining Company. When Knot finally made it official, many people in the communities of Daggett, Barstow and Yermo were excited to know what the future held for the old silver town. Soon, they knew, as Walter Knott had big plans for the old town. Calico would once again become the jewel in the Mojave Desert.

3.

THE LEGEND OF LUCY LANE

No history of the town of Calico would be complete without the story of Lucy Lane. Lucy lived in Calico longer than anyone and epitomized the spirit of the town and those who lived and died there. She was the eldest of the four children of George and Laura King. Lucy's father left Los Angeles for Calico in 1884 and sent for the rest of the family in 1885. The Kings built a small family home in East Calico, where George was working. Lucy was only ten years old when she was brought to the town, and she positively loved the hustle and bustle of the main street. As Lucy wrote, "I was intensely interested and loved the activity in the town and district of about 3,500 population, for Calico was booming with miners coming and going."

The Kings would go into town and shop at Joe Miller's General Merchandise Store, and they would purchase enough goods there for a whole week. The goods would then be delivered to them by the store clerk, John R. Lane. Lucy's mother constructed furniture for their new home by using items they had lying around from the move, and she also constructed a desert cooler out on the porch and had ice brought in to act as a "refrigerator." The four kids would split time doing the chores and exploring the colorful hills that surrounded their house. Laura King would bleach the flour and sugar sacks to make summer underwear, and she taught Lucy how to crochet and trim their clothes; Laura had her learn how to use the sewing machine during her summer vacations from school.

John and Lucy Lane. *Courtesy of the Mojave River Valley Museum.*

Early life wasn't easy for young Lucy. When her mother was asked to take over the Bismarck Boardinghouse after its Chinese cook suddenly left, Lucy had to wait on tables along with completing her other chores and schoolwork. To get to school, Lucy had to walk a mile and a half over King Mountain while carrying her schoolbooks and lunch pails and wearing hobnailed brogan shoes. Every once in a while, a wagon would come by, and if the girls were lucky, they would be offered a ride over the hill. One day, they saw John Lane driving a wagonload of goods to East Calico; he offered them a ride, and they laughed the whole way, as the wagon bounced them around due to its heavy load. Apparently, John Lane enjoyed the trip as well because, on every delivery to the King house following this, he would bring a bag of candy for the King children.

As Lucy and her siblings grew, their father allowed them to sort through some of the tailings as a way to earn some money and stay out of trouble. Their first profit came to two dollars and was split between the four of them. They continued to collect and sort the dump soil, and by Christmas, they had earned enough to buy new clothes from a Sacramento catalogue.

In 1887, Lucy's father decided that a school in Sparda, California, near Pomona, would better prepare his kids for high school, so he sent them with their mother to attend the schools there. The Kings lived in Sparda for only two years, and then, because of medical advice for Mrs. King, they moved back to the desert for her health. When they arrived, there was a knock on their door, and when Lucy's father opened the door, John Lane was standing there, having just come back from mending a pipe at the Calico Schoolhouse. Lane visited for a while, and his company was much enjoyed, but after he left, Myrtle said, "I think he is the homeliest man I ever saw." Lucy, for her part, completely disagreed but didn't say anything out loud. Shortly after this visit, John Lane moved back to his home state of Georgia.

After finding that the wages there were lower than they were in the California desert, Lane moved back to Calico and brought the new mining techniques he had learned in the South. There, they used water to power the machinery and to wash the ore down to the mill; this new technique greatly reduced the cost of the mining operation and allowed Lane to buy the water company in Calico. Lane also bought a large two-room cabin across the street from the King home. John Lane began spending evenings at the King house. As Lucy's mother explained it, "It was natural that John, being a southern man, should spend time at a southern woman's family home." Mrs. King invited Lane over for Thanksgiving dinner, and the gathering lasted well into the morning hours, with singing and fun had by all. Then, when the Christmas Tree Program was held in the courthouse, John Lane accompanied the King family, and they all made wreaths, decorated the tables and had a wonderful Christmas dinner with those in attendance.

In the spring of 1891, Lucy celebrated her sixteenth birthday, and after dinner, John Lane asked Lucy to go for a walk with him. During their walk, John gave Lucy a scarf pin for her birthday, and as he pinned it on her, he said, "When you put on long dresses, I will propose to you." A year later, on Lucy's seventeenth birthday, her mother made her first long dress. John Lane was there to see her put it on, and afterward, he again asked Lucy to walk with him. Lane asked Lucy if she remembered what he had told her the previous year, and when she said she did, he proposed. Lucy was scared that he was sixteen years older than her, but she agreed to marry him when she turned eighteen. After John and Lucy were married in 1893, John bought a store in town, and that, along with his other holdings in and around Calico, allowed the Lanes to live a simple but comfortable life.

As the orders for deliveries grew and more money was at hand, John and Lucy began investing in many of the area's mine holdings. The Lanes became fixtures in Calico, and everyone in town knew that if they needed anything, the Lanes were happy to help. John would deliver goods to homes in the surrounding area, and if the residents were short on money, John would gladly extend a line of credit. The Lanes not only became storekeepers but friends to most in Calico.

Over time, as the price of silver continued to decline, the need for credit grew. Many of the miners were out of work or digging through mines that couldn't produce enough to support them or their families. Through it all, the Lanes were there. As payment for their debts, some of the miners turned over their interests in the Silver King Mining Company. John Lane filed suit against the Silver King; the suit was dragged out for years but was finally settled in John's favor. But as the miners were moving out of Calico, the Lanes were forced to close their store, and they boarded up the house to move into their mill, where John continued to work his mines. In 1901, the Lanes moved to Glenn Ranch, where John took a job as manager and Lucy waited on tables and learned to milk cows, make butter, can fruit and raise chickens. After leaving Glenn Ranch, the Lanes moved around, going from San Bernardino and Los Angeles to Rhyolite, Nevada. But no matter where they were, Calico always beckoned. So, in 1916, as the price of silver began to rise slightly, the Lanes moved back to Calico and opened up their mining interests once more.

Their return to Calico came as a shock. Most of the buildings in town had been torn down and moved to Otis, which had changed its name to Yermo; many of the mills that they had once used in Daggett and elsewhere had been sold, and the town was nothing but a shadow of what it had once been. They had to live in their old store building, and while John went out to mine, Lucy did her daily chores and used a wash bucket to pan tailings for its quicksilver. John was finally able to hire someone to do this, which allowed Lucy to concentrate on her homemaking duties. Life was hard for a while after the Lanes moved back, but when silver again reached a value of one dollar per ounce, things improved. The town itself still hadn't recovered, but visitors were starting to arrive, and John and Lucy were happy to show them hospitality and teach them about Calico and its history.

When John passed away in 1934, things changed for Lucy. She began splitting her time between Calico and the town of Julian. As she grew older, she found the extreme heat to be bad for her health, and as she had friends living in the San Diego area, she thought the change would do her good. Calico was all but abandoned, and when Lucy was there, she was mostly by herself. Visitors still came, and she still enjoyed giving them all a warm

John and Lucy Lane are buried side by side in San Jacinto, California.

welcome. When the movie studios began to arrive and use the town as their backdrop for westerns and other films, Lucy was there, offering to cook meals for them at a reasonable price. When others began to move back into town and open up tourist shops, Lucy helped them get established as best she could. When Walter Knott purchased Calico from the Zenda Mining Company, the same company that bought it from the Lanes, Lucy was there. As the new tourist town of Calico was reborn, Lucy Lane was there to make sure it was done right. After the town opened up as a county park, Lucy remained and continued to greet guests, as she had done so many times in the past. After her death, Lucy was buried next to her husband in the town of San Jacinto, California.

Lucy Lane lived in the town of Calico from 1885 until her death in 1967. Lucy was not just a resident of the town, she was its symbol, the personification of the American mining spirit and of those who went before her. Lucy Lane was Calico, and for those who believe, Mrs. Lane is still looking after the town she loved.

4.

A MINE IS A TERRIBLE THING TO WASTE

The first known mining operation to start up in the Mojave Desert near the town of Calico was the Oro Grande group of mines, which sprang up about five miles east of the town of Victorville. This gold mine was established by Judge William Clancy, along with his partner H.H. Markham, who was a retired army colonel. When the Silver King claim was found, the silver brought out of the mines had to be transported through town, down into the dry lake and hauled across the desert for forty miles, to the Oro Grande Mills. This caught the attention of Markham. After seeing the rich ore coming out of the Silver King, Markham took out a lease with an option to buy for $60,000 and began digging new holes for the Silver King Mines. Once Markham realized just how rich the silver ore was, he took up the option to buy. He didn't have the cash to buy the mines outright, so he made a deal to pay for it over time, using the silver ore itself as it was produced. The ore was so rich that it averaged $110 per ton for a year after production began.

The Waterloo Mine grew to the west of town and became one of the largest and, arguably, most famous mine in the Calico area. The mine employed so many men that it erected a large store where the miners could trade for the goods they needed to live. The Waterloo Mining Company actually compelled its employees to shop at the trading post, but the company did offer a train ride from the mines down to the store free of charge.

The Waterloo Company shipped its ore to the stamp mills near the town of Calico Junction, along the south side of Elephant Mountain. At first, the

The Silver King Mine ore bin. *Courtesy of the Mojave River Valley Museum.*

ten-stamp mill was adequate for the company, but as the Waterloo Group had a larger vein with a lower-grade ore than most of the other mining groups, it was decided that a larger mill was needed. A new sixty-stamp mill was built in 1886. At first, it was an arduous task to get the ore down to Daggett (Calico Junction's name was changed to Daggett in 1883 to avoid confusion when it was granted a post office; it was named in honor of then-lieutenant governor John Daggett, who owned mining interests in the Calico area); it took three days for the round trip to the Calico mines and back to the mills. Twenty-mule team wagons hauled supplies to Calico and Borate and brought the ore back down on the return trip. (The famous twenty-mule teams were started when ten teams were hitched together with two wagons and a water wagon followed by a long flatbed wagon.)

For a brief time, an experiment took place in which a giant steam tractor named *Old Dinah* was used to pull the ore and borax wagons in an effort to cut costs in manpower, wagons and mule tending. Unfortunately, the steam tractor required constant maintenance, and it had trouble navigating deep sand and going up hills. It was said that *Old Dinah* would slide backward faster than it moved up the hills, and that driving it was like going backward instead of forward. *Old Dinah* lasted only a year before the twenty-mule teams were reinstated.

In 1888, the Oro Grande Milling Company began what it called the Calico Railroad. The line originally went from the Oro Grande Stamp Mill

"Old Dinah." *Courtesy of the Mojave River Valley Museum.*

to the Waterloo Mines but was extended to the Silver King Group in 1891. When the extension was completed, there were over one hundred tons of ore being shipped daily from the Silver King Mine and another fifty tons from the Waterloo. Each steam locomotive pulled five open cars and a water tank. Each train made five trips daily, filled with ore from Calico, and then loaded with lumber, explosives, detonating caps, powder and fuses, along with more mundane supplies, for the town itself. As the price of silver declined, the cost of operating the rail line grew, and the Daggett–Calico Railroad was closed down in 1892, four years before the mines were closed.

Tensions between the different mining companies arose; many arguments were over mining rights, apex disputes and claims. One of the worst in Calico was between the Runover Mining Company and the Waterloo Mining Company. The trouble began when the Silver King Group, which was owned by Waterloo, dug a new vein that ran up against the Oriental No. 2, which was owned by Runover. The Oriental then gained the apex rights to the vein. After the Runover Mining Company found rich ore, the Waterloo Group tried to claim the land. The court case lasted quite some time, with the Runover Mining Group winning

Above: One of the ore trains that ran from Calico to Daggett. *Courtesy of the Mojave River Valley Museum*.

Opposite: Sue (Sioux) Falls. You can just see the ladder leading up to the mine's adit at the end of the canyon. *Courtesy of the Mojave River Valley Museum*.

a $300,000 judgment. During the lawsuit, the townsfolk nicknamed the Sliver King Group the "Lion," while the Runover Mining Company was known as the "Lamb." The case, however, had more far-reaching consequences beyond the courtroom.

On April 26, 1885, a dance was hosted by the Odd Fellows. During the dance, two employees of the Waterloo Mining Company began tossing eggs at the miners employed by Runover. As the eggs landed and the targets dodged them, two gunshots rang out, causing everyone to scatter, looking for cover. Women began screaming, while two actually fainted and had to be taken outside to recover in the fresh air. When the commotion died down, the dance continued. No one was taken into custody that evening, but the next day, a Mr. Marlow was arrested and fined fifty dollars. Marlow had been hired by the Runover Mining Company to act as a guard for its employees attending the dance. In the area where the miners had to work, the Silver King miners, being above those of the Oriental No. 2, allowed waste rock to fall down around the miners working on the slopes below them. Naturally, this bred some deep animosity between the two groups of miners. Another dispute arose between the Occidental No. 2 and the Thunder Mine over

the Thanksgiving Fraction Claim. This dispute got to be so bad that the miners had to come up from the mines carrying guns; so, it became known as the Shotgun Raise.

Working as a miner was never a safe proposition. Many of the adits (mine openings) were high above ground level or on top of cliffs and mountain tops. One example of this was the Sue (Sioux) Mine's adit. This mine sat one hundred feet high above Sioux Falls. The only way to reach its adit was to scale a ninety-two-foot ladder that followed the slick walls of the dry falls; one had to hope their grip was steady and firm. The biggest danger for miners by far wasn't climbing ladders or being blown off of high, windy ore chutes; it was the constant and ever-present threat of cave-ins.

On June 6, 1891, there was a cave-in at the Waterloo Mine. James B. McGowan was killed in the collapse. At first, rescuers thought he may have survived, but as the search for McGowan dragged on, it was clear that he had perished in the cave-in. McGowan's body was never recovered. When a miner went missing, the loss of a loved one was hard for the family that remained. When the body was never found, it was devastating. This was made very clear by Margaret Oliver one night, when she related the tale of how Jimmy McGowan's mother reacted to her son's death.

After the cave-in at the Waterloo Mine, where Jimmy McGowan perished, relays of miners dug frantically, trying to rescue him until the danger became too great for their lives. His poor mother thought when the wind blew down the canyon it was her son moaning in his lonely grave. She almost went insane, so they left Calico.

John Hoban said of McGowan's remains, "The Waterloo Company sent a lovely white casket for his burial if his body should be found." Jimmy McGowan's body was never found, and the casket was in the Lane Store for a number of years. While it was there, people actually slept in it. The casket was finally moved to Barstow by druggist Gene White. White also ran a funeral parlor and most likely sold the casket.

Another deadly collapse happened at the Silver King Mine in 1909, when a shaft ceiling came down, killing Matt Phillips. There may have been only one death, but it brought into specific relief the ever-present danger of working as a miner. One other death was notable, as it reminded everyone that collapses were not the only things that could bring danger to the mines. On June 24, 1895, while trying to free damp ore from a chute in the Oriental Mine, Mr. W.G. English climbed into a manway to pry the ore loose, and

A Calico miner posing outside of the Jack More Mine, one of the many mines in and around Calico. *Courtesy of the Mojave River Valley Museum.*

although his attempts were successful, when the ore broke loose, it crushed English, killing him instantly. English was buried in the Calico Cemetery.

As mining towns go, Calico had a pretty good safety record, even though it did have its share of mine mishaps. It has been said by more than one miner working in the Calico mines that the reason for this was the abundance of Tommyknockers that inhabited the dark spaces the men worked in. There were many who believed the stories of these mythical fairies were nothing more than nonsense, but more still believed that to ignore the Tommyknockers was dangerous at best and suicide at worst.

The legend of the Tommyknockers came to the United States in the early 1820s, when Cornish coal miners immigrated to this country. Since mining was an ancient profession for the Cornish people, they gravitated to the coal mines of Pennsylvania when they arrived in America. It was in this region that the Tommyknockers established their foothold in the American mining scene. Then, as the Cornish miners moved west, they became highly sought after by the mining companies in the western states for their experience as master miners, and the Tommyknockers moved with them. It was a long-held belief among the new immigrants that a race of fairy creatures, similar to the Irish leprechauns, lived in the mines and worked, unseen, right alongside their human counterparts. Tommyknockers are described as being two feet tall with greenish skin and a look similar to gnomes. The Knockers are believed, in Celtic society, to be kin to the Irish leprechauns and English brownies. German miners were also familiar with these impish creatures and called them *Berggeister* or *Bergmännlein*, meaning "mountain ghosts" or "little miners."

There are many theories about the origins of these creatures among believers, and they range from the idea they are the souls of the Jewish people who crucified Christ that were sent by the Romans to work the tin mines to the idea that they are the ghosts of miners who died in mining accidents that were transformed into fairy creatures and sent to guard other miners as they worked the mines. Whichever theory one believes to be the beginnings of the Tommyknockers, most believe that they look out for other miners. Believers say that these small men live in the dark recesses of the mines and that, the deeper one goes into the earth, the more likely one is to run into one of these little miners. The Knockers were said to be a very private folk and disliked it when humans came into their habitats, but it was also said that they would work side by side with the human miners, invisible and unknown, when they were working in the areas of the mines that were deemed "community" areas. There were times when miners would break for the day, and when they would return to the mines the next morning, they would find the section they had been excavating cleared and the veins either found or the area eliminated as a looking place. The miners, of course, credited the Tommyknockers.

The Knockers were also quite helpful in other ways. When a miner lost their tools, they would often come back from looking for them just to find them sitting next to their lunch bucket or water jug. New candles and lanterns and tools miners had left at home would suddenly appear when miners needed them. Minor courtesies were one thing, but the Tommyknockers' help went much deeper than finding lost equipment or completing mundane tasks. The Knockers were also known to save the lives of countless miners around the world over the centuries.

Most miners believed that the Tommyknockers had good intentions—at least, mostly good. When miners heard the telltale *tap, tap, tapping* on the ceilings of the shaft, they knew it was the Tommyknockers warning of an imminent collapse and that they needed to get out fast. Others thought that the tapping was the Tommyknockers themselves banging away at the support beams in an attempt to kill their human counterparts. Either way, the miners who believed in the little gnomes would heed their warnings and get out of the mines as quickly as possible. Those who didn't believe in the Knockers would inevitably laugh at their superstitious coworkers and continue working. These miners would often be found under tons of rubble, and if they were still alive, many would become full believers in the tales of the Tommyknockers.

The belief in the Tommyknockers was so great in many of the mining camps that it became common practice for miners to bring extra food with them in their lunch pails to leave out for the Knockers. Also, when the miners went home for the day and met at the local saloon, they would leave a space at the bar for the Tommyknockers in case they decided to join them for a drink. Miners have always been a superstitious group; from worrying if their clothes slipped off of their hook that they would fall into a hole to thinking their wife was having an affair if their lamps went dim, miners always worried. One of their worst fears was of red-headed women entering the mines. Women were bad enough omens, but redheads were considered omens of death. This belief in women as bad omens makes the fact that one of the most successful single owner mines was owned by a woman rather ironic.

Miners sitting around outside a stone-front saloon in Calico. Many of these miners would buy drinks for the Tommy Knockers as a way of thanking them for their camaraderie and protection. *Courtesy of the Mojave River Valley Museum.*

As the price of silver kept dropping, the one thing that kept Calico alive was the borax found in the hills nearby. It was in the winter of 1882 and 1883 that Hugh Stevens extended his prospecting and found white crystals that looked like quartz but wasn't as hard. Stevens sent a sample to San Francisco that confirmed it was borax. Stevens claim was eventually sold to Francis Marion "Borax" Smith. Once Smith bought the claim, he spared no time in setting up a camp in Mule Canyon. This camp became the small mining town of Borate. At first, the town was no different than its neighboring town and began with miners living in tents, caves and frame bunkhouses that Smith erected for them. The main difference was that the Borate miners worked for the Pacific Coast Borax Company rather than their own claims. Borate was a company town; along with the wooden bunkhouses, Borate consisted of a dining hall, company store, reading room and small cabins for the storekeeper and the mine foreman. Smith also had a large home built for himself at the head of the canyon. The house, which was not well planned, sat atop a rise. Every time the winds picked up, the house would shake, rattle and threaten to come loose from its foundation. It got so bad that steel cables had to be attached to anchor the home to the hillside or it may have blown over.

Borax Smith was not only an accomplished miner but a shrewd businessman. To help his company grow, Smith used the twenty-mule teams

A master at advertising, "Borax" Smith turned the twenty-mule team rig into a multimillion-dollar advertising campaign that is still used and known today. *Courtesy of the Mojave River Valley Museum.*

The "Puffer" locomotive *Francis* was used to haul borax from the town of Borate to the roasting plant in the town of Marion. *Courtesy of the Mojave River Valley Museum.*

that hauled his minerals as his official logo; it also became the brand name of the product that still bears the Twenty-Mule Team name today. The Twenty-Mule Team brand became so famous that a 1932 article in the *Los Angeles Times* called borax from the Pacific Borax Company "million-dollar dirt." Smith marketed borax as having "100 uses," from toothpaste and cold cream to enamel and cookware. Borax was also known as an exceptional cleaning product and is still in widespread use today.

As popular as the logo was, the mule teams were a slow and costly way to get the mineral to its destination of Daggett. So, in 1898, the Borate and Daggett Railroad was built. Constructing this line was not easy, as it traversed some steep terrain and unforgiving landscapes. "Puffer" locomotives hauled the ore cars along the tracks via two legs; the first leg, from Borate to the Marion Roasting Plant, was run by the steam locomotives *Francis* and *Marion*, which were named in honor of Francis Marion Smith, and the second leg traveled from Marion to Daggett.

An interesting chapter in the town of Borate and Calico occurred when a temperance organization based in Oakland found out that Borax Smith only allowed his miners three hours off on Sunday. They demanded Smith give the men the whole day so that they could attend church. Rather than receiving bad publicity, Smith relented, and he told his foreman to see to it. When Sunday arrived, the men, knowing that the nearest church was in

San Bernardino, headed instead for the Alec Falconer's Saloon in Daggett. It wasn't until the middle of the week that all of the crew arrived back in Borate for work; by that time, Smith had already canceled Sunday as a full day off. The cancellation of their Sundays off caused the miners to go on strike. This slowed down production at the Marion Roasting Plant, but it didn't stop it.

When a rumor was started that a mining crew was coming into Daggett on the afternoon train, a group of miners went down to meet the scabs when they arrived. As the train pulled in, a single passenger got off, wandered over to one of the miners and asked what all the fuss was about. "The miners have lost their Sunday afternoon off, and they have struck," came the reply. The conductor called out all aboard, and the passenger, Tom Conniff, who was a former night foreman at the mine, shook his head, got back on the train and continued on to Arizona, where he was headed for work. This event ended the strike, and a few days later, all of the men were back at work. This was the only strike at the Calico Mining District in all the years it was in operation, and thankfully, it was a short and peaceful one.

Borate may have been the largest borax facility in Calico, but it wasn't the only one. There were borax operations in the Odessa and Bismarck Canyons, along the northeastern hills of the Calico Mountains and the hills just beyond Yermo. The Yermo group was sold to an Englishman who

With the desert reclaiming Calico, there wasn't much left of the town when Walter Knott purchased it. *Courtesy of the Mojave River Valley Museum.*

eventually incorporated it as Borax Properties Ltd. This company grew to employ 125 men; it also dug a mile-long tunnel with a tramway and even built a number of houses. The mill the company built was completed in 1907, just before the Banker's Crisis (also known as the Knickerbocker Crisis) of 1907 hit. The banking crisis signaled the end of borax mining in the Calico district. As the price of borax plummeted to three cents, Borax Properties Ltd. closed down its operations, and most of the smaller mines shut down. When a new deposit of borax with a high concentration of colemanite (another borax mineral) was found in Death Valley, the Pacific Coast Borax Company closed down its mines in the same year and moved all of its operations back to Death Valley.

With all of the silver mines closed down and the borax mines shutting down as well, Calico had finally become a ghost town. Lucy and John Lane were all that remained until the Zenda Mining Company bought the town. But even Zenda couldn't save Calico from being reclaimed by the harsh Mojave Desert. Through it all—the town's glory days, its rapid decline and short rebirth in the borax era and its inevitable abandonment—one person marked the time, one person bore witness to the rise and fall of California's official Silver Mining Town: the indomitable Lucy Lane.

5.

DORSEY, ONE HELL OF A TAIL

This legend is one that can warm the heart and define just how true the statement that dogs are man's best friends is. The tale has become a bit more romanticized over the years of its retelling; this is most likely as a result of the 1977 Wonderful World of Disney television movie *Go West, Young Dog*, as well as the Kenny Rogers 1972 hit, "Dorsey," from his *Ballad of Calico* album. There is also a 2010 children's picture book titled *Calico Dorsey, Mail Dog of the Mining Camps* (by Susan Lendroth, published by Tricycle Press on September 28, 2010) that may also have played into the kinder legend we know today.

The story goes that, one day, Calico postmaster Everett Stacy found a stray border collie laying on his porch. Stacy, unable to find the dog's owner decided to keep it as his own. Everett named his new pup Dorsey, and the dog's reputation grew among the townsfolk—that reputation wasn't a good one. The people of Calico thought the dog was nothing more than a lazy animal who constantly came around, begging for food and loafing around any shady spot he could find, usually Stacy's front porch, until the next handout came his way.

The mail would come into Calico by stagecoach every day, and Stacy would sort out the letters and correspondence that was to be sent on to East Calico. Everett's brother, Olwyn, owned a store in the town of Bismarck, which was about three miles east of Calico, and the post office for the town was in this store. So, every day, Everett made the trek along the steep, rocky dirt path to do his duty and deliver the mail to the other town.

Everett didn't like it, but it did allow him to see his brother, and he was a dedicated government employee. After Everett adopted Dorsey (Dorsey was originally named Jack and was known as Jack, the mail-carrying dog, by the *Calico Print*, according to a May 10, 1885 article), the dog became his companion on the delivery trips to Bismarck, and the town became quite familiar with the dog as a result, and apparently, Dorsey became familiar with Bismarck as well.

One day, Everett Stacy needed to get an urgent message to his brother, but because he wasn't feeling well, he knew he wouldn't be able to carry it himself. Stacy somehow knew that the message needed to get to his brother, so he decided to send Dorsey with a note in the hopes that the dog knew the way well enough to get there on his own. Stacy wrote out what he wanted to say, attached it to the dog's collar and then pointed the dog in the direction of the other town and loudly told him, "Bismarck!" Dorsey looked at his master, hesitated and then began walking in the direction of the other town. After a few hesitant steps, Dorsey turned back to Everett and started to turn back, but a sharp, "No, Dorsey, go to Olwyn," was enough for the dog to finally get the idea, and he bounded off down the dirt path heading east. That was the last Everett saw of the dog that day. Not knowing if Dorsey had made it to his brother or if the dog had gotten lost, attacked by a wild animal or had just decided to wander away, Everett turned in for the night and hoped for the best.

The following morning, there was still no sign of Dorsey, and Stacy figured that the dog had wandered off. However, as Stacy opened the door to head for the post office, there was Dorsey, waiting on the porch with a note from his brother. The dog looked like he had been treated nicely, was well fed and seemed no worse for the wear. This gave Everett the idea to see if the dog might be able to deliver the mail from time to time to the other mining camp. To this end, Everett Stacy began training Dorsey to carry more and more mail, along with packages, and instructed his brother, Olwyn, to send back any outgoing letters or correspondence. Dorsey took to the task like the town drunk took to the local saloon. This was the start of the legend of Dorsey, the mail-carrying dog.

This may not be the truth of the tale, however. Lucy Bell Lane, a longtime resident of Calico who, as a child, knew Dorsey and the Stacy brothers well, differed in her account of how the dog began his mail duties. In her book *Calico Memories* (published by the Mojave River Valley Museum and Alan Baltazar in 1993), Lucy Lane said:

Among the early timers in Calico were two brothers, Everett Eli Stacy and Olwyn Stacy. Eli was postmaster when we arrived. He had a jewelry store in front of the building, while the post office was in the rear. Early one morning in 1885, Mr. Stacy found a black-and-white shepherd dog shivering on his doorstep. As no one claimed the dog and he seemed intelligent, Mr. Stacy decided to train him.

One day, his brother, Olwyn, who had the post office in connection with a grocery store at the Occidental No. 1 Mine in East Calico…came to town. He [Olwyn] *petted the dog and played with him. After he* [Olwyn] *started home over the trail, he noticed the dog had followed him. Olwyn thought he would tie a note to his brother around the dog's neck and send him back to Calico by giving him a few lashes with the whip. The dog struck out across the trail for Calico.*

The dog was renamed Dorsey for a famous mail carrier of the early days. The two brothers decided to train the dog to carry the mail, so Olwyn tied a note around his neck at Calico and, showing him the whip, started him over the trail to East Calico's post office. When the dog reached the post office, Olwyn took the note from his neck and gave him food and water. It was decided the dog would stay in East Calico.

As you can see, the true story of how Dorsey became a mail carrier is not the pleasant, feel-good story that has grown out of the dog's legend. However, it doesn't take away from the amazing career that Dorsey had while performing the duties he took to so well. The rest of the story seems to be close to the truth, and it is one that should remain as a true tale of man's best friend.

The brothers made a special satchel for Dorsey to carry the mail. The bag was draped over his shoulders, with a pouch on either side and straps going around his chest to keep the satchel securely in place. With this system in place, the dog began his daily trek of three miles over to the Bismarck camp and returned the following day. After about the first week, however, the Stacys noticed that the dog's paws were starting to show signs of injury. The rough stones and dirt, mixed with the heat of the desert sun, were taking its toll on Dorsey's feet. The brothers had a set of booties made for Dorsey; the leather shoes made the trail much easier for the dog, and as an added bonus, Dorsey was able to make the trip much quicker.

Dorsey was becoming a town celebrity, and the miners and townsfolk of both Calico and Bismarck treated the dog as such. Dorsey had several stops along his route; they were not official stops, but miners who knew Dorsey's routine would be out waiting for the pooch and would give him cuts of meat, strips of jerky and other treats. This way, the miners got their mail without having to go into town. The dog began to know which houses he could get these treats from, and he would always make sure to stop.

News of Dorsey began to spread outside of the Calico Mountains, and it wasn't long before a string of newspaper articles and photographs began appearing all over the country. Photographers began appearing in town, and they all wanted to snap pictures of the amazing dog and the miners in the area. Those who wanted to be a part of the growing legend began buying up the pictures so they could put them up on the walls of their cabins and homes. In 1886, the *San Francisco Chronicle* ran an article that is indicative of the stories that were running all over the United States. It said, "He [Dorsey] is immensely popular with the miners, whose mail he carries so faithfully, and every evening at Bismarck, the miners order extra beefsteak for the canine carrier." Dorsey was becoming larger than life, and his adventures were spreading far beyond what the reality of his job entailed.

Dorsey was steadfast in his ability to get the mail where it was supposed to be, and when a stranger or another dog appeared on the trail, Dorsey would give them a wide berth and continue on his way. There was only one time that Dorsey failed to get all of the mail to its proper destination; although, this may be one of those stories that was told to add color to his legend. It is said that when Dorsey arrived back in East Calico one evening, Olwyn noticed that one of the dog's bags was open. Upon inspection, Stacy saw the remains of some wrapping and noticed what appeared to be cookie or cake crumbs still in the package. Olwyn looked at Dorsey, scolded the dog and thought he noticed the dog acting guilty. No one complained about missing mail or missing cookies, so the Stacys let the incident go with just a warning to the hungry pup.

As cost effective as Dorsey was for delivering the mail, Dorsey's days as a mail dog only lasted a little over a year. The Stacy brothers had other plans for their future, so when the brothers decided to move away for greener pastures, Dorsey was forced into retirement. Just because the Stacys were leaving Calico, they weren't abandoning Dorsey. The brothers were acquainted with one of the owners of the Bismarck Mine, Mr. W.W. Stow, and they knew just how much affection Stow had for Dorsey, so they approached him and asked if he would take the dog to live with him in San Francisco. Stow readily agreed. Dorsey lived out the rest of his days in comfort, living in the Stow Mansion, and meals were served without him needing to walk a daily mail route.

One of the only known pictures of Dorsey, the "mail-carrying dog." *Courtesy of the Mojave River Valley Museum.*

Dorsey may not have exactly led the fantastic life that his legend and stories portray, but no one can say that this amazing animal didn't leave a lasting impression on those who knew of him. Perhaps the best epitaph for this lovable and incredibly intelligent dog came from Lucy Lane when she wrote:

> *When Dorsey was off duty, we children romped and played with him. If he was carrying the mail, no one but the two postmasters could touch him. He often passed us on the trail when we were going to school, but we never tried to pet him when he carried the mail. Dorsey brought something lovable and warm into the lives of us children.*

6.

KNOTT YOUR TYPICAL GHOST TOWN

Walter Knott, the creator of Knott's Berry Farm, California's first themed amusement park, worked in Calico as a younger man. His short stint at the slowly dying town had a profound impact on Knott that stayed with him until his death in 1981.

Walter Knott was born in 1889 to a small family. His father was a preacher who unfortunately died when Walter was only six years old. At the time of his father's death, the Knott family, which included a father, mother and two sons, was living in the town of Pomona in eastern Los Angeles County. Being a single mother with two young boys wasn't financially easy, so to help make ends meet, Walter's mother took a job with a laundry service. It wasn't long before Knott began working as well. Walter took jobs delivering newspapers and cleaning the local church once a week, and he began growing vegetables for the family to make sure they had enough to eat. Walter was a good farmer, and his crops began producing more than the family could eat, so Knott began selling the extra vegetables to his neighbors and townsfolk.

Walter loved farming. He loved the feeling of growing things and feeding people. As he grew older, he dreamed of owning his own farm and would often tell anyone who would listen that he would own farmland someday. Even though his mother tried to talk Walter out of quitting school, Knott left high school after his sophomore year to go to work picking melons. Walter saved most of his money, and after only a short time, he had enough to buy his own land in the Coachella Valley. Since the land was in the desert near Palm Springs, California, it was not really suited for farming, but Knott, never one to give up, persevered and managed to earn enough to make a small profit.

After he was unable to make enough to keep his farm going, Knott returned to Pomona. Walter began working as a cement contractor and began courting a girl he'd had his eye on since high school, Cordelia Hornaday. The two fell in love and were married; Cordelia then gave birth to their first child, Virginia. The Knotts were getting along just fine, but Walter still dreamed of being a farmer and owning his own land. When Knott heard about homesteading opportunities in the Mojave Desert, he contacted the U.S. Land Office and found out that if he picked a parcel of land and spent three years living on it, the land would then be granted to him. Walter immediately put in his application and was granted a 160-acre parcel of desert that was approximately twenty-five miles east of Barstow, California. This suited Knott just fine, as he was already familiar with the nearby Calico Mountains.

It took a bit of convincing to get Cordelia to agree to the move, but when she finally relented, Walter bought a cow, some chickens and two horses, and the family moved out to the arid wasteland of the Mojave Desert. Since he

Walter and Cordelia Knott standing next to the commemorative bust that was erected in their honor in Calico. *Courtesy of the Mojave River Valley Museum.*

had been told by people in the know that a deep well for water was a must, Knott hired a crew to dig one. But with the well constantly filling with sand and his money running out, Knott decided to take matters into his own hands, and he hand dug a shallower well himself. This smaller well was barely adequate and had just enough water for the family to fill buckets to irrigate the small number of grape vines they were able to grow. Unfortunately, as it often happens in desert environments, a sandstorm came on the farm and uprooted the vines that Walter had so carefully cultivated.

While the Knotts tended their land in the Mojave Desert, near the town of Newberry Springs, Cordelia gave birth to two more children. The financial strain on the family caused Walter to take odd jobs around the area, helping out new settlers in their efforts to homestead. Even with the extra work, the Knotts found their money situation less than desirable, so Walter, keeping an eye out for opportunities, jumped at the chance to take a carpenter's job in the nearby town of Calico. Knott was very familiar with the small mining town in the hills, as his uncle John King was one of the founding partners in the Silver King Mine, and he had grown up listening to stories of the Wild West that his grandmother told him while visiting his uncle in Calico. The Silver King Mine became the largest producer of silver ore in Calico and was responsible for the boom the town saw in its early days.

This is the way Calico looked when Walter Knott began restoring the town. *Courtesy of the Mojave River Valley Museum.*

Walter worked as a carpenter in the town, but as the economy was gearing up for World War I, it didn't take long for Knott to be put in charge of his own crew. During this time, Walter lived in Calico, away from his family; it was just too far to travel home each night, and Walter, working as hard as he did, was just too tired to make the trip. Without anything better to do, Knott wandered the town in the evenings, exploring the abandoned structures. Seeing all of the personal items left behind by the former residents and remembering the town as a child made Walter Knott fall in love with Calico. Even as his love for the town grew, his responsibilities to his family were still the most important thing in his life. When a higher-paying job with a road crew became available in the area, Knott jumped at the chance. Reluctantly, Walter left Calico, moved back home to Newberry Springs and began helping construct Route 66, the Mother Road.

Even after Knott left Calico, he never forgot the town or his love for it. His life was still an up-and-down roller-coaster ride of financial hardships and struggle, but Walter never gave up on his family or his dream of being a successful farmer. The Knotts lived on the Newberry Springs homestead for three and a half years. This was long enough for the 160 acres to become their property, and it remains in the Knott family to this day. When the Knott family finally settled in the farming community of Buena Park, California, their fortunes had improved. Walter knew that the time for him to fulfill his lifelong dream had finally come, so he bought the town he had come to love. Calico was his.

7.

THE LEGEND OF CALICO CEMETERY

The one thing that every old Wild West town is known for is having a Boot Hill, and Calico is no exception. But there is something a bit different about the Calico Cemetery that sets it apart from many other burial grounds. That difference is that no one really knows how many souls are interred here; this is mostly due to the abandonment of the town itself.

After the silver and borax ran out and the town was all but forsaken, the cemetery became a prime location for grave robbers, souvenir seekers and desert dwellers who needed wood for everything from building material to firewood. Because of this, fences and wooden markers were removed, and headstones were carted off; others were simply vandalized, and many graves were dug up in search of jewelry, coins and other items that could bring the grave robbers some money. Once people began to return, albeit slowly, to Calico, it was discovered that, with the loss of the grave markers, the graves themselves had been lost to the wind and ravages of time in the desert. They had been damaged to the point that it was impossible to tell where the original graves had been laid. Officials began looking for records from the town, and even though they found some, they were not detailed enough to really figure out who all had been buried there while the town was populated. The closest estimates that authorities can come up with say that the cemetery holds between 117 to 130 graves.

To make matters worse, once Calico was restored by Walter Knott in the 1950s and early 1960s and then turned over to San Bernardino

Calico Cemetery today.

County to become a tourist attraction, it was discovered that not only was the graveyard in complete disarray and in need of protection, it needed complete restoration as well. This was one area that seemed to have been overlooked by Knott and those tasked with the town's "de-ghosting." Once San Bernardino Rangers began looking for those who were actually buried in the cemetery, they discovered that there were quite a few fake grave markers within the boundaries of the graveyard. Names such as Wyatt Earp (who had been to Calico but was buried in Colma, California), Doc Holliday, Kit Carson and Billy the Kid, along with other Wild West notables who had never set foot in Calico, were represented at the cemetery in an attempt to lure tourist traffic to the town.

In the 1970s, the first true attempt at finding out who was actually buried in the cemetery began. Investigators began combing through death certificates, burial permits and coroners' reports, and they even went looking through the personal stories of those who had lived in Calico. This all produced some results, but it still only confirmed that the 117 people who were already believed to be buried in the cemetery were there, and only about 20 percent of those people were properly identified. It wasn't until the 1980s, when infrared aerial photos were taken, that it was discovered that at least 160 bodies were buried at the cemetery. With these photographs, historic pictures and the personal accounts that had been gathered earlier, investigators were able to produce a map with a rough estimate of where the graves were actually located. Unfortunately, even with all of this new evidence, officials were still only able to identify 49 of the approximately 160 bodies in the cemetery.

It is believed that the first person buried in the cemetery was a thirteen-year-old boy named Bobby Stephens. This young lad was actually buried there in 1869, before the cemetery—or the town, for that matter—came into existence. It is believed that this may have been one of the reasons the cemetery was placed in its current location after the town was created, but no one knows if that is the case.

Calico was a rather peaceful mining town, unlike others, such as Bodie, which had a reputation of hosting daily gunfights and murders. Calico, even with its many bars and brothels, had very few murders. Even with this peaceful history, there are still a couple of bodies buried in the cemetery that have sordid stories attached. One such tale is the murder of a popular man by the name of Anastacio Rubio. After arriving back in Calico from an ore delivery, Rubio had decided to head to his favorite saloon, where he

The early Calico Cemetery, with no fence or border and markers made of wood and stones. *Courtesy of the Mojave River Valley Museum.*

began treating his friends to a round of drinks. Rubio had six dollars' worth of silver and eighty dollars' worth of gold in his pocket, and it wasn't long before he had blown through the silver and produced the gold to buy another round. This caught the attention of another patron, who, when Rubio left the saloon, followed him out. Once outside, the robber, who was described in the *Los Angeles Herald* on June 2, 1883, only as "an American," shot and killed Rubio and then relieved him of his gold. Even though the murder took place just outside the saloon, a lack of witnesses allowed the murderer to go free. Three days after his murder, Anastacio Rubio was buried by some of the miners in the Calico Cemetery, but his grave remains unidentified today. He may also be one of the restless spirits that is found in the graveyard; this may be due to his violent death and lack of justice for his murder.

Many people might find it hard to believe that, in a rough-and-tumble mining town like Calico, those who worked their knuckles to the bone in the pursuit of wealth also had hearts of gold. This next tale goes to show that even the toughest of Calico's men had soft spots for their fellow human beings. In 1896, a mining broker from Los Angeles by the name of Albert Roland was in Calico on business and had decided to take a break from work when he hit up one of the local gambling halls, the Dickerson and Mosely Saloon. Roland and another man, Ed Scollard, had gotten into an argument, but the two men had been cooled down by the other four miners whom they had been playing cards with. As the game continued, it was obvious that Scollard and Roland were still not getting along, and about an hour after their first argument, another ensued. This time, however, the two men could not be calmed. *During the altercation, Scollard pulled out a revolver and struck Roland across the face with it. Roland then pulled out a small pocketknife. Even though Roland didn't open the knife, this caused Scollard to fire one shot, which struck Roland in the chest. He died a half hour later. Scollard was eventually tried and convicted of murder, and he spent the next seven years in San Quentin Prison. Roland was only twenty-five years old at the time and left behind a widow and two young children. When Roland's family arrived in Calico and the miners found out that his wife and kids were left destitute, they immediately took up a collection to help pay for the funeral, and they gave Roland's wife one hundred dollars. Roland remains in the Calico Cemetery today.

---

* Author's note: There is some confusion about this story. One report from July 1896 states that Scollard was trying to break up a fight between Roland and another man when Scollard drew his revolver and shot Roland.

Just one of the many dilapidated grave markers that are still in the cemetery.

One of the more adventurous, albeit lawless, stories about an interment at the Calico Cemetery involves a man by the name of Harry Dodson. Dodson was a former millworker for the Runover company. He had been out of work for a while, and with his prospects of work getting thin and his wallet thinner, Dodson became desperate. On September 10, 1889, Harry Dodson rented a horse with the supposed purpose of going out to look at a mine. Instead, Dodson rode over to the Runover Mine and robbed its superintendent, James Patterson, at gunpoint. After stealing the estimated $4,395 payroll (roughly $112,692 today), Dodson also stole Patterson's horse. He then made his way out into the desert, to Hawley's Station, where he could rest and hopefully wait out the furor over his crime.

The next day, Patterson, a saloon owner by the name of John Ackerman and a native tracker named Tecopa John formed a small posse and went looking for Dodson. They didn't have to look long, however, as Dodson had become hopelessly lost out in the desert and had been riding around in circles in a vain attempt to get away. Dodson's—or, in actuality, Patterson's—horse had gone lame and Dodson, was on foot, leading the horse. The posse caught up with the robber at Coyote Wells, a muddy watering hole. When Dodson saw the three men approaching, he pulled his Smith & Wesson .44-caliber pistol and opened fire. The posse, armed with a Colt .44 and a Winchester repeating rifle, returned fire. When the gun smoke settled, Dodson had holes behind his left ear and through the left side of his chest, near his heart. The young would-be robber was dead. Harry Dodson's body was brought back to Calico and buried in the cemetery.

In 1888, a diphtheria epidemic swept through Calico, and unfortunately, the disease killed several children in the town. As the schoolhouse had been moved from the lower section of town to the upper area, many of the kids had their funerals near the school; this may be the cause of one of the more prolific ghosts in town and this will be discussed later. Once a funeral was complete, a solemn procession carried the children down to the cemetery, where they were laid to rest. Unfortunately, many of the children's graves have since been lost, but we do know that Eva and Bruce Cochran, the daughter and son of William and Emma, the couple who ran the boardinghouse, were buried there, along with Robert Stevens and Earnest Rowe. Although the children's graves have become lost with time, many of the piles of stones in the cemetery are much smaller than those that cover adult graves, so it is likely that there are children buried under them.

There are other markers within the Calico Cemetery that we do know are not what they appear to be. Some may be left over from the days when

One of the colorful characters buried in the cemetery.

people saw gravestones with names of famous cowboys and gunslingers and others may just be practical jokes left over from workers or those townsfolk with a penchant for the odd. Others, it would seem are actual graves from those who lived in town at the time but are still unusual from who or what is buried there.

One of the more obviously fake tombstones that is still in the cemetery is that of Daisy Dooly. The tombstone reads, "Daisy Dooly 1887. Came to town one day and wasn't long before she was led astray. She's in a better place today, we pray." This epitaph seems to imply that Daisy was led into prostitution when she arrived in Calico. Now, even though we know that the "soiled doves" of Calico were a necessary part of mining town life, we also know that this tombstone is a fake that was created in the 1950s by rangers trying to attract tourists. The legend has not only persisted over the years, but it has, in fact, grown. The humorous nature of the rhyming tombstone leads one to wonder if Walter Knott himself may have had a hand in its creation. After all, it is reminiscent of the rhyming markers in the Knott's Berry Farm Boot Hill, which say, "Here lies Sonora Jim. To a tall tree he was risen, the pinto he stole wasn't his'n," and, "Here lies Poker Face Harry. A whiz at cards called hearts, fast at draw poker. Too slow once to draw, that was the joker." Knott had a knack for dramatic humor and could very well have been the culprit who created Daisy.

Another tombstone that may be a bit of a prank is someone's actual resting place. However, even though we know a body is buried there, the name on the marker, Blackie Scroggins, seems to belong to a person who never existed, at least not in Calico. No record can be found of anyone who went by that name, especially a claim jumper, which the marker claims Scroggins was: "Blackie Scroggins, claim jumpers take note." Yet another of these most-likely fake markers is that of Wes Wescott. Mr. Wescott was supposedly hanged at Calico, but unfortunately, no one by this name could

Calico did have its share of interesting personalities.

be found as having ever lived or died in the town. The epitaph on the marker says, "Hung in his youth, t'was a sad mistake when we found the truth." Again, the similarities between this amusing epitaph and those at Knott's Berry Farm are hard to overlook.

Another interesting aspect of the Calico Cemetery is that there are more than just humans buried there; although no one would ever guess this by simply looking at the gravestones and markers. There is a marker that reads "Tom Kate and Tom Kate Jr." By looking at this, one would think that a father and son are buried here; however, the bodies buried in the grave are those of two tomcats—not humans at all. Then, there is the marker for Bruce Wallin. This child died at the age of eight, according to the grave marker. Did he die during the diphtheria epidemic or some tragic accident in town or in the school yard? No, as it turns out, Bruce was actually the Wallen's dog who died in 1944 and was originally buried in a cemetery in Yermo. Sometime in the early 1950s, the dog was moved to the Calico Cemetery.

Other notables who have been interred at the Calico Cemetery include Samuel King, who helped found the Silver King Mine; Margaret Olivier, who was the Calico schoolteacher in 1898 and 1899; and "Tumbleweed" Harris, who was perhaps the most loved street performer Calico has ever known. There is even a man interred there named John Dent, who committed suicide by drinking himself to death—his alcohol of choice is not mentioned on his grave marker.

There are Boot Hill Cemeteries all over the West. Gunslingers, cowboys, lawmen and "soiled doves" are all buried within their hallowed grounds, and many of these cemeteries are now as famous as the towns they serve. Many more have been lost to time, as the shanty towns and mining camps have vanished, and Mother Nature has reclaimed her land. Some believe there is no other cemetery that has seen the amount of controversy or legendary fame for its lost graves than Calico has. Is it any wonder that legends say that restless spirits wander among the graves and beckon the living to rediscover them and their remains so that they can be remembered by those they left behind?

8.

CALICO RESURRECTED

With Walter Knott growing a healthy crop of new berries that would come to be known as boysenberries, and with Cordelia running a successful restaurant, serving chicken dinners with all of the trimmings and wonderful berry and fruit pies for dessert, he felt that he needed a way to keep the growing crowds entertained while they were waiting in line to eat dinner. His idea was to create a small Wild West town that his guests could explore and learn from. He had always wanted a way to educate people in the ways and hardships of American pioneers, and the town would be a way for him to do just that. Knott started with an old hotel he purchased from Prescott, Arizona, and over the next ten years, he acquired a blacksmith shop, jail, schoolhouse, stagecoach and paraphernalia from towns around the West. By 1951, Walter Knott had enough capital to realize his boyhood dream, and he bought the town he loved so much— Calico Town was his.

At the time the Knott family purchased Calico, the town was already attracting some tourism. The small, nearby town of Yermo held a yearly festival at the end of May called Old Calico Days, and this brought a modicum of interest to the ghost town. Residents Harold and Lucile Weights began producing a tabloid-style newspaper titled the *Calico Print*, in honor of Calico Town's first newspaper, as a way to not only help inform the locals of happenings in town and abroad but also as a way to get tourists interested in the town. Even with this small, renewed awareness of Calico, the town had been neglected for so long and it was in such a state

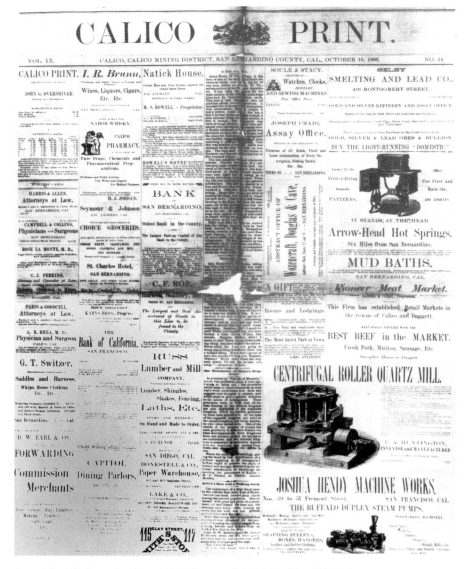

An original Calico print from 1886. *Courtesy of the Mojave River Valley Museum.*

of shambles that Knott knew it would take a lot of work, time and money to bring the ghost town back to any degree of prominence.

One of the first things that Knott did was hire Fred Noller to oversee the rebuilding—or de-ghosting—of Calico Ghost Town. Fred was a well-traveled man, as he had been a miner, cowhand, mariner (he sailed around the world) and artist. Fred even spent some time in the Chinese Second Army. But none of this really mattered to Knott. What stood out to him about Fred was that he knew about the history of western towns and that he looked like he had walked off of a Universal Studios Wild West movie. Knott also brought in artist Paul von Klieben to help make sure that Calico looked like a Wild West ghost town. Klieben had been working with Knott for many years and was the one responsible for how the Knott's Berry Farm Calico Ghost Town looked. Knowing what a success the amusement park town was enjoying, Knott knew that Klieben was the man to help Noller create the perfect atmosphere in the real Calico Town. Klieben was often seen wandering the hillsides, overlooking what remained of Calico; he was always framing in his mind the designs that he had planned for the recreation of the town. He then drew out his blueprints and submitted them to Knott for approval. Once the plans were finalized, it was time for Noller to get his crews working on the designs.

The "de-ghosting" and reconstruction didn't always go as planned. Having grown up in the Arizona desert, Noller knew what the winds could do to the buildings and structures after long years in the hot, arid and windswept desert landscape. Walter Knott was aware of the effects as well, and since he wanted Calico to represent the true picture of a desert mining town, he agreed with Noller that it should look as authentic as possible. This wasn't always popular with the architects and builders hired to do the work, however. A story written in the *Santa Cruz Sentinel* on February 21, 1955 (by Graham Berry in volume 100, number 44), summed up the problems this effort had on some of the crew.

"Throw the T-square away!" Ordered Fred Noller, his long fingers drumming on the holster of his .45. "You've got to make that porch roof and pillars lean."

"Lean?" Exclaimed the incredulous carpenter. "Which way?"

"The way the desert wind would have blown her over the years," explained Noller, his shaggy goatee waving in the breeze.

He leaned his six-foot-plus frame against a pillar and shoved until the porch's three uprights and roof were noticeably out of plumb.

"Now, nail her up," commanded Noller, who enforces what probably is the strangest building code in the country.

The carpenter gulped. "On one condition," he said. "Promise you'll never tell anyone I did it."

Noller nodded. The job was done.

That evening, the carpenter packed his tools, got in his car and drove off down the Calico Mountains, towards Barstow, never to return.

"Had a lot of that kind of trouble up here." Complained Calico Fred Noller. "Not many journeymen can put up buildings according to ghost town standards."

Fred Noller and his wife, Gladys, lived in Calico in a small house located to the south of town while they oversaw the restoration. They became so intertwined with the town that Fred picked up the nickname of "Calico Fred." When he was not busy looking after the restoration, Fred would walk around town, talking to and entertaining the tourists who came to see a real Wild West mining town. Fred became the town marshal and was often seen on one of the hilltops overlooking Calico, keeping a watch over his town, usually with his dog, Miner, by his side.

One of the jobs Fred was tasked with was inspecting and closing off mines that may have been unsafe for tourists. Noller had to enter the mines on occasion—never a safe proposition—to determine what to do with it and how to close it off. On one of his trips down a shaft, Fred found a dog struggling to survive and unable to get out. Apparently, the dog had fallen into the mine and would have died if Noller hadn't found him. It was a bit of a struggle to get the pup out, as Fred had to hold onto the dog while ascending a ladder; he finally tied a rope around the animal while straddling the hole in a precarious fashion and hauled the dog up to safety. From that moment on, the dog was named Miner and never left Noller's side.

Fred Noller's wife, Gladys, didn't just sit at home and wait for her husband to get home from a hard day's work; she liked to help out at the tourist stores that had opened in town. She could be found stocking shelves, waiting on customers or lending a hand in any of the shops that needed help. One of Gladys's favorite shops was the Assay Office. This shop was first operated by George and Ginny Dotson; it sold polished mineral jewelry and single stones that the Dotsons had gathered from the desert floor and hand polished. The store, which was housed in the original assay office for the town, also provided information to its guests on the local minerals and where to find them. Miner the dog could often be found at Gladys's side, lending a helping paw.

Paul von Klieben, on the other hand, was the farthest thing from a Wild West character that one could be. Born in Austria in 1895, Klieben emigrated to the United States in the early 1900s. As an artist, Klieben wanted to paint scenes that depicted real life in the western half of the country, and

Knott, Noller and Klieben would use photos like this to re-create Calico's buildings from its heyday. *Courtesy of the Mojave River Valley Museum.*

he wanted to show how the Native Americans and others had lived in the Wild West. He caught the attention of Walter Knott in 1938, and Knott, impressed by the artist's talent, immediately hired him to finish a mural at Knott's Berry Place that had been started in honor of Knott's grandmother. After seeing Klieben's work on the mural, Knott hired him as the resident artist and designer at his burgeoning amusement park.

Klieben was the driving force behind many of the original buildings at the Calico Ghost Town of Knott's Berry Farm; some of them had actually been taken from photographs of Calico Town itself. There is a myth that says Knott dismantled many of the buildings from the actual town, transported them to Buena Park and reconstructed them for his amusement park. This would not really have been possible, however, considering there were very few buildings left in Calico at the time Knott bought the town. After Walter Knott purchased Calico Town, it was an easy decision for him to put Klieben in charge of the building design and placement in re-creating Calico itself. The artist could often be found on a hilltop or vantage point overlooking Calico, formulating his

Today, the Bottle House is a small souvenir shop. Knott built it as a testament to the pioneer spirit of perseverance.

design concepts for the buildings he would need to erect and planning the restoration of those he could save.

Klieben and Knott often got together in Calico; Knott took on a personal and hands-on approach to the restoration process. The two men often took trips to other ghost towns, Bodie and Rhyolite chief among them. One of the most famous additions to both Calico and Knott's Berry Farm's version of the town was the Bottle House. Klieben and Knott found this gem at Rhyolite, and even though it has no historical connection to Calico, the town was known for using "alternate" building materials for structures, and this building seemed to fit in well within that theme. Although it was built to a smaller scale, the Bottle House at Calico was constructed out of 5,419 bottles of varying sizes and colors. It has become one of the most well-known attractions in the old mining town. Today, the Bottle House is a small shop that sells souvenirs to guests.

9.

THE LEGEND OF DIAMOND LIL

Paul von Klieben was one of those people who strove for absolute authenticity whenever possible. Because of this, Klieben thought that having a hostess to greet visitors at the old mining camp would help get guests into the spirit of the Old West. They couldn't be just any hostess, however; to Klieben, the only acceptable choice was a person who looked as much like a local legend as possible. She had to be the embodiment of Diamond Lil. The tale of Madame De Lill had been circulating around Calico for as long as anyone could remember. Paul von Klieben had been hearing about it from not only those who lived and worked at Calico but many visitors to the town who were constantly asking if the stories were true.

The story says that Madame De Lill owned the largest saloon on Main Street. De Lill always said that she didn't move to Calico for her health or to strike it rich, but one thing was for sure, De Lill knew how to run a saloon. She not only had the largest saloon in town, it the best saloon as well. One of the things that made Lil's saloon stand out was that she would take high-grade ore as payment from the miners. They could buy just about anything for a lunch pail full of ore. Tobacco, liquor, pool games, booze and even girls were available. Things were going well at Lil's until she made the mistake of falling in love with one of her partners. Bill was one of the more handsome men living in Calico at the time; he was large, muscular and always impeccably dressed. Unfortunately, he was also one of the more shady and insincere characters in town. Lil and Bill had an extremely short courtship and were quickly married at the church with great fanfare; there was also much sadness from the single ladies living in Calico (Bill, you see, was very popular with the ladies).

After they were married, Bill became a regular fixture at the saloon. With his wife as the owner, Bill would sit at his table as if it were a throne, telling tall tales and handing out free drinks to those he held court with—especially the women who came to listen. At first, his tales and antics were good entertainment for the crowd, but his constant loud and drunken repetition of his stories became more obnoxious with each retelling. With that, coupled with Bill's womanizing and cheating, Lil had enough of her philandering husband and came up with a brilliant way of getting him to leave her and Calico for good.

De Lill realized that if she didn't get her husband to shut up, he was going to drive away business and she would go broke. So, one night, she approached Bill to tell him to be quiet. Bill, being in his usual state of drunkenness, began to argue with his wife, stood up and announced to the crowd, "[I'm] going somewhere I will be appreciated," and walked out of the saloon. De Lill's husband didn't stagger home until almost sunrise, and he went straight to bed, passed out and began snoring. De Lill promptly grabbed Bill's revolver, emptied the chamber of all of its bullets and replaced them with blanks. Her plan was set in motion from that point on. The next morning, Madame De Lill enlisted the aid of a very large, three-hundred-pound Swedish miner by the name of Big John. After telling him of her plan, he agreed to pass the word on to a few other miners who would be in on the scheme. That night, when Bill arrived, De Lill would finally be rid of her obnoxious, drunken husband—or so she hoped.

When the time came, Lil's saloon was packed with miners. After Bill had a few drinks in him, he began retelling his same old tales, so Big John walked up to him, called him a liar and slapped him hard across the face. Stunned, Bill reached for his pistol but didn't pull it from its holster. John glared down at Bill and slapped him again. This time, the crowd called out for Bill to "shoot that damn Swede." Others called out, "Let him have it," and still, others urged, "Kill him, Bill." The crowd kept calling for Bill to kill the big miner until Bill finally stood up, pulled his gun and fired three shots into Big John's chest. The Swede hit the floor, grabbed his shirt and pulled it open trying to get to his wounds, but the blood pouring out of his chest made it impossible to find the bullet holes. Big John squirmed on the floor, his face oddly twisted with pain; he looked up at the people staring down on him, and with one final "He got me, boys," Big John died.

Bill stood there, looking in horror at what he had just done and watched as the oddly colored blood poured out onto the saloon floor. The crowd went silent until someone approached Bill and whispered, "Get out the side door, or it will be a necktie party for you after shooting an unarmed man. I'll meet you at the cemetery in five minutes with a horse and enough supplies for you to get far away from this mess." So, with the help of a few other miners, Bill managed to escape out of the side door of the saloon and was soon seen racing on horseback toward the town of Daggett. Bill was never seen in Calico again, and he never sent word on what to do with his shares in the business, so of course, De Lill kept them for herself.

As Bill made his escape, the crowd back at Lil's began to laugh. As Big John rose from the floor, trying to wipe off the red ink that he had stolen from the mine superintendent's office, De Lill congratulated him for his superb acting. John, on the other hand, thanked De Lill for making sure Bill's gun, which he had dropped to the floor, had been loaded with blanks. The whole scam had worked like a charm, and Bill was out of De Lill's life for good. De Lill never remarried, and Diamond Lil's Saloon remained the largest, best and most-profitable saloon in Calico until the silver prices plummeted and the town was finally all but abandoned in 1896. No word of what happened to Bill has ever come forward.

Of course, this story is unverified; however, Paul von Klieben thought there was enough truth to the tale that, in 1951, he sent a letter to De Lill, who was believed to be living in Tombstone, Arizona, at the time, asking if she could send a picture of herself from that time period so that he could, "Recreate Diamond Lil by selecting a girl as hostess of the camp who, in her appearance, comes closest to your person in the Days of the Calicos." It is not known whether Klieben ever received a response.

10.

CALICO COMES ALIVE

The restoration of Calico was a long and sometimes hard process. Many of the original buildings had burned down, blown down or they had simply rotted away in the harsh desert sun. With Paul von Klieben designing various buildings from old photographs and paintings or from seeing representative structures from other mining ghost towns, along with "Calico" Fred Noller overseeing the restoration and his vision of what an old mining town should look like, Calico began to live again.

One of the first structures to get attention was also one of the most important—at least to those who lived nearby—because it was owned by the last living resident of Calico; this structure was the Lane Mercantile Store. This store was opened by John and Lucy Lane after they were married in 1893. Lucy had lived in the town of Calico off and on since the age of ten. Calico became their permanent home in 1916, and they made the store's building their home until 1920, when they moved into the old courthouse and post office building. Lucy lived there until 1965, and she passed away two years later at the age of ninety-three while living in Virginia City, Nevada. The Lane Mercantile Store is still open to this day.

Klieben and Knott knew that many of the buildings that had once stood in Calico could never be duplicated. To this end, they scoured old photos and other ghost towns for ideas on how to create authentic western buildings. As the aforementioned Bottle House was an easy choice due to its unusual properties, other structures needed to be of a more mundane nature. One of these was the old schoolhouse. Luckily, there were plenty of photographs of

Calico's second schoolhouse, and using these, a replica was built at the same location, just outside of town, but it is one-third smaller than the original structure. Even though this is a replica building, it has become a hot bed for paranormal activity.

Another building that was erected on Main Street was a two-story structure that was modeled after the Cosmopolitan Hotel, which stood there in the 1880s. This building was originally used as a candy store. Unfortunately, like often happens in mining towns, the structure was burned to the ground in 2001, but it was later rebuilt.

Other structures that were built or rebuilt in Calico by Walter Knott were the C&H Smelter building, which has mainly been used as the blacksmith's shop, showing authentic tools and hosting demonstrations of the work, and McCulloch's Supply Warehouse, which also burned in the fire of 2001 and was subsequently rebuilt. As mentioned before, fire is the bane of all towns that are made primarily of wood. One of the things Knott built was a wood-frame firehouse. The building serves as a museum of sorts and features a La France Company fire engine that was built in 1896. Another Knott original was the Top O' Hill Bazar. This building was designed for merchants and was opened in 1958 by Walt and Rose Applebury as a souvenir shop. Walt later became the town marshal.

Walt also added the Lucille Mining Company Tram. This narrow-gauge railway ran between the Wall Street Canyon parking lot and up the steep hill to the Main Street station. The visitors to the town who wanted to walk could ascend a trail punctuated by switchbacks that was designed to help alleviate the extreme grade and arrive near the same Main Street station. Another

Calico, circa 1967. This is how Calico looked when Walter Knott turned the town over to the County of San Bernardino. *Courtesy of the Mojave River Valley Museum.*

This is all that remains of the tram from the lower parking lot to the town above.

railway was also constructed in Calico; this one, however, was built more for fun than necessity. The Calico and Odessa Railroad was also constructed by the Lucille Mining Company and was a narrow-gauge rail line built to take passengers on an excursion through the canyons and hills of the surrounding area that were normally not accessible to casual visitors. Riders were taken across a one-hundred-foot-long trestle that spanned Jackass Gulch, past the old mine shafts and the multicolored Calico Hills. The railroad was begun in 1957 and completed a couple of years later. A small railway depot and ticket office were built near the old Maggie Mine, and once it was completed, this ride became one of the most popular attractions in Calico—it still is today. Both the tram and Calico and Odessa Railroad were owned and operated by Shafe-Malcom Enterprises. Boyd and Margaret Clark were the on-site managers when the attractions were opened to visitors.

Mules had always been an important part of any mining town. These beasts of burden were used to help transport the building materials that were needed for not only town construction but for shoring up mine shafts and keeping them from falling on the miners' heads. Mules would transport ore back to town and would bring back the needed wood, mining tools and equipment, along with food and water for the men working the mines.

The Calico-Odessa Railway Trestle.

Anywhere a mining operation was found, one could also find mules. Calico was no exception. Mules were even used in the reconstruction of the town; because of this, Knott wanted to make sure visitors were made aware of the importance of these animals. To this end, a burro corral was built just below the Maggie Mine in Jackass Gulch, next to the ruins of the old Chinatown structures. Guests could wander over to the corral, see these wonderful animals and, if the burros were willing, pet them when they came near the railings. They could even view foals on occasion.

The Mystery Shack was one of the most visited attractions in Calico and was born from an idea Knott had to add a bit of intrigue to the town. First constructed at the upper end of Main Street, this area allowed guests to experience optical illusions up close and personal. Visitors could marvel as a small child stood next to their father and appear much taller. They could also watch as water seemingly flowed uphill or gape at a woman who appeared to stand at an angle that should have made her fall to the ground. The crowd could oftentimes be seen leaving the shack shaking their heads in wonder. The original Mystery Shack burned to the ground in the fire of 2001, but it was quickly rebuilt in its current location in town.

Not everything in the newly refurbished town was built by Knott. The Lane Mercantile building is an original, but it was so dilapidated by time and neglect that an extensive refurbishment was needed. The Maggie Mine building was redone, and the mine itself made safe and opened to visitors to explore. The Calico Print Shop structure was another building that needed widespread repairs, but when it was operated by Ray Milligan in the 1950s and 1960s, he gave copies of the original *Calico Print* to visitors to read. Milligan would also help out around town by printing out many of the storefronts' signs. Rhea's Drug Store, the Assay Office, the Zenda Gold Mining Company buildings and others were refurbished and put into use as shops or for guest services. Even the old, two-door, rammed-earth outhouse that remained from the 1880s was refurbished. The last building constructed in Calico during its final restoration was the Calico House Kitchen. This restaurant, when it was opened, was run by Joe and Jean Lopez. The establishment sold a variety of food, including sandwiches, entrées and, as was reported, a "very tasty strawberry pie." The Calico Kitchen has now become the longest continually operated business in Calico Ghost Town.

The whole time that Walter Knott rebuilt Calico, he allowed visitors to come and explore the town. Since Calico had been lost and mostly forgotten, many would-be visitors found the town hard to locate. Knott decided that the best way to help direct guests was to put signs up along the

One of the original buildings that was left in Calico when Knott bought the town. Rhea's Drugstore has now been repurposed as Diamond Lil's Saloon.

roadway leading to town. Knott erected a sign near the main road and the turnoff to what is now Ghost Town Road that told people that Calico was "3 miles up the road." The sign also had a giant arrow pointing visitors in the right direction. The sign told folks that the town was free to enter and that it was being "restored by Knott's Berry Farm." Knott figured it couldn't hurt to advertise both his amusement park and its connection to the mining town. Once people arrived in the parking lot, signs directed them to both the walkway and tram, along with information about the town itself. However, no amount of advertisement could compare to the now-famous sign, which was painted in white lettering at the top of King Mountain and simply says, in giant letters, "Calico." This sign, which was painted in 1959, has become so well known that it is actually used as a navigational aid for local air traffic.

While Calico was being restored, one could not help but feel the history and flavor of the old mining town. Once the major restoration was complete, Walter Knott wanted to make sure that feeling wasn't lost to his visitors. To help keep that atmosphere alive, Knott placed various symbols around town that would make guests think about where they were. One of these reminders, which was put up in the 1960s, was a glass-sided, horse-drawn hearse. Often referred to as a Black Maria, after the hearse at Boot Hill in Tombstone,

Arizona, this static display became one of the more popular attractions in town, as people were anxious to get a look at the coffin inside. Another relic that was placed in the town was an old, wooden water wagon; this, Knott hoped, would help make people realize that early desert communities were dependent on wagons to bring them life-sustaining water. If the water wasn't available, it could have spelled immediate doom for those living in the town. A similar wagon was also used as a billboard outside Calico, showing the way to the town.

Knowing how the visitors to Knott's Berry Farm enjoyed the shows and spectacles there, Knott figured that he should do the same in the original Calico. Since the Calico and Odessa Railroad

The first sign you see when exiting Highway 15 on Ghost Town Road. Notice the name Calico is high up on King Mountain to the right of the marker.

was up and running, it was decided that a more natural way of travel, one that was more historic to the hills, needed to be established. This was accomplished by a man named Don Hughes, who created Uncle Don's Burro Train. Recognized by his bushy white beard and red underwear, Uncle Don led guests through the Calico Hills while riding burros. This attraction and Uncle Don himself were so popular that, after Uncle Don passed, he was buried in the Calico Cemetery.

Of course, "Calico" Fred Noller was also seen wandering around town, his marshal's badge ever visible; at least, that was until 1958, when Walt Applebury took over that "job." And then there was the Cactus Corral. This cactus garden was open for the public to wander around in and marvel at the various cactus plants there. Caretaker Ted Hutchenson once quipped that it was "the one place in Calico where you could really get stuck." Hutchenson even put up a sign for guests that said, "Please feel free to touch all you want."

Lucy Lane still lived in Calico during and after the restoration period, and she could often be seen sitting out in front of the stores. She was always gracious with those who came up to talk to her, and she loved telling tales about the old Calico. But perhaps the most beloved character to walk the streets of Calico during this time was "Tumbleweed" Harris. Donald Willard "Tumbleweed" Harris was one of the more noteworthy characters who worked in Calico Ghost Town. Harris originally worked at Knott's Berry Farm; he added color to the made-up town there. Once Calico was completed, Walter Knott asked him to be a part of the town staff. Harris was thrilled to work there. Tumbleweed loved working the crowds that came to visit, and he loved the people he worked with even more. He could always be seen wandering around town, telling folks tales of the Old West. Harris became one of the most beloved characters to both the guests and employees.

Born in New Jersey, Donald Harris grew up and fell in love with the mystery of the Wild West. After he moved out west, he took a series of odd jobs, always moving around, always in a different place. One thing that didn't change for Harris was his love for the desert. More than one of his friends quipped that he could always be seen wandering all over the desert, just like a tumbleweed. This was said so often by those who knew him that he was forever dubbed "Tumbleweed" by his friends. The day before Tumbleweed died, a photograph of him was placed in the Calico Town Hall; he was one of the first to be so honored. Harris had requested to be buried in the Calico Cemetery, and he requested those who worked

"Tumbleweed" Harris was perhaps the most beloved character actor in Calico. He has a prominent plot in the Calico Cemetery. His ghost is also said to still be in the town.

in Calico to wear their street character costumes when they attended his funeral. Everyone employed in Calico attended the funeral, as did many of his friends from his days at Knott's Berry Farm, and everyone wore their garb in honor of Donald Tumbleweed Harris. Tumbleweed loved the town of Calico so much that, according to staff and guests alike, he is still present in the town today.

With the restoration of the town complete, Walter Knott began the legal procedures to turn Calico over to San Bernardino County. Knott figured that, with his amusement park, Knott's Berry Farm, growing and the boysenberry farm itself taking up so much of his time, the county was in a much better position to keep the old silver mining camp alive for generations to come. One of the stipulations that Knott incorporated into the contract with the county was that San Bernardino had to always maintain the town as a tourist attraction and museum or ownership of Calico would revert back to the Knott family. This part of the contract has become a point of dispute, with many people saying it was never included and others saying it is still in effect; still, others claim it has been amended and is no longer enforceable. Whatever the case may be regarding the

Walter Knott turned Calico over to San Bernardino County in November 1966. *Courtesy of the Mojave River Valley Museum.*

Calico Ghost Town today.

agreement between Walter Knott and San Bernardino, the town was officially turned over to the county in November 1966.

After San Bernardino County took over the town, it decided to expand its tourist draw. Unfortunately, because of this, the town took on the appearance that guests thought a Wild West town should have rather than what a Wild West town would have actually had. The county brought in street performers to put on an "authentic" Wild West gunfight between the sheriff, his posse and a band of outlaws bent on bringing havoc to the town. It expanded the Maggie Mine so that guests could explore and get a feel for what mining was actually like, and it modernized the signs that show the way to town. The county also added a camping ground and RV area so that adventurous tourists could have a place to enjoy the town right on the grounds of Calico itself. For those folks who weren't campers or RV enthusiasts, the county built cabins and a bunkhouse, where the more luxury-minded could stay, albeit in understated luxury.

Today, San Bernardino maintains Calico as it always has, with seasonal street performers, souvenir shops, sweet shops and other specialized curio stores, along with shops featuring the stones and gems that are prevalent in the Calico Mountains. The Calico and Odessa Railroad still takes guests on an easy and delightful excursion through the hills and canyons surrounding the town, while the Mystery Shack still amazes those who venture inside. But most of all, Calico still gives those who visit a glimpse into what life was like when settlers searched for riches, looked for love and survived in the hostile, arid Mojave Desert.

11.
MINING AND DINING THE SPIRITS

A s ghost towns go, Calico isn't the largest, most well-known or most historically accurate; in fact, Calico is now more of a tourist town than a ghost town. With a bookstore, photo studio and rock shop, along with rides and attractions, it is sometimes hard to tell if you are at Knott's Berry Farm's Calico Ghost Town or the original mining town. Although Knott's Berry Farm has its share of ghosts in its Calico, the actual silver town in the desert is teeming with spirits. Whether these ghosts are starving miners or people who just love the smell of the eateries and concessions in the ghost town, many of them like to hang out in the restaurants and food stands throughout the town. So, if dining with ghosts is on your bucket list, Calico Ghost Town may be the place to go to check it off your list.

LIL'S SALOON

Although Lil's original saloon is gone, Calico has done what it is best at and has repurposed another of its original buildings to house a watering hole, where guests can get hotdogs, slices of pizza and cold sodas and beer. The new saloon is located in what used to be Dr. Rhea's pharmacy and office. There is some speculation that Dr. Rhea's ghost may be one of the spirits that occasionally makes itself known in the saloon, but no one is quite sure who the ghosts may be.

One of the more common occurrences reported in Lil's is the sound of a phantom poker game. These experiences usually occur after the eatery has been closed for the night and the employees are busy cleaning up after the day's customers have gone. Even though the place wasn't originally a saloon, after its conversion from an old pharmacy, many of Calico's character gunfighters would go to Lil's after performing to have a cold beer and play a few hands of poker to entertain the guests. It is believed that the spirits are these men who have returned to continue their games of chance. Many times, employees will be in the back and hear the sound of chips being tossed on the table, glasses being put down and cards being dealt, along with the sound of hushed conversations and laughter. Since they know the saloon is closed, these employees emerge from the back room, expecting to see other town employees or guests, but they only find the main room empty and quiet. Many times, after going back to work, the sounds return, only to have the same result if the room is checked again. Employees who have worked at Lil's for any length of time have learned to ignore the sounds or, if it becomes bothersome, ask the spirits to keep it down, at which point, the ghosts usually quiet down.

In Bill Cook's book *Ghostly Guide to Calico Ghost Town* (published by Magic Valley Publishers in 2008), he tells a story about an experience that occurred on one of his ghost tours outside of Lil's. Cook said that, one evening, as he was telling guests about the history of the saloon, a picture behind the beer taps began glowing in an eerie blue light. As he had never seen this before, he went to Lil's the next day to ask about the effect they had put on the picture. He was told that there was no blue light or special effect, and Bill just forgot about it. A few months later, while he was leading another ghost walk, it happened again, but this time, Bill knew it was most likely spectral. No one is sure why the picture glowed in a spooky blue, and as it has not been reported since, one can only speculate. But if you feel like grabbing a hot dog, a beer and a spook, then Lil's Saloon is the place for you.

OLD MINERS CAFÉ

Sitting at the top of the town—or what is currently the top of the town—across a wash within sight of the schoolhouse, is the Old Miners Café. This eatery isn't an original building, but if you're in need of a sandwich, burger or cold soda that comes with a great view of the Calico Dry Lake and part of the town of Daggett, this is the spot for you. Not only will you get a good burger and great view, you just might get to meet one of the town's former residents.

You don't have to wait until you get to the café to have a paranormal experience, however. The bridge leading from Main Street that is directly across from the Sweet Shop is said to be home to a number of spirits. It is said that, in the days Calico flourished, the town had a number of red-light districts and brothels; one of them, a mobile brothel, was said to have been set up under the bridge every now and again. It wasn't a bright idea to set up such an establishment in a wash that could flood during a storm, so the brothel was erected during the dry season and then would move to a different town during the other times of the year. Be that as it may, many strange tales have come from the café bridge.

One of the most common reports is the sound of women's laughter coming from just below the bridge as people cross to the café. This mostly happens during dusk, around the time that Calico is getting ready to close for the day and while guests are rushing across the bridge to get their last soda or snack before their long drive home. These sounds are often accompanied by the sudden and strong scent of perfume that seemingly comes out of nowhere. The perfume is usually that of rose or lavender, two scents that the ladies of the evening would use in abundance to mask the scent of their previous customers if they didn't have time to bathe before seeing their new client.

Under this bridge, there was a mobile brothel. It is said that the ladies may still be there, plying their trade.

Some people have even claimed to have heard full conversations coming from under the span, but when they look to see who is under the bridge, there is no one to be seen.

At the Old Miners Café itself, employees working in the eatery have reported hearing sounds from the main room while they are back in the grill area. Thinking that there is a customer waiting, they come out, only to find that there is no one there. One employee said that, once, while she and a coworker were doing some chores in the back, they heard what sounded like a couple having an argument. It was nothing serious, just a disagreement over where they were eating and what they would order, but it was enough of a spat to get the employees' attention. Hoping to quell the dispute, the employees hurried out to take their order and found that the place was empty. One of the employees went to the front door and the patio door, but there was no sign that anyone had been there. She quickly went back to her coworker to confirm that he, too, had heard the quarrel, and after he said "yes," they were both confused by what they thought they had heard.

The small storeroom in the back of the kitchen also seems to have a fair amount of spiritual activity. Stories have been told about phantom noises that come from this area near the grill as if someone is moving things around or looking for something. Employees who have gone to check on the area have found cans, produce bags and other items moved from where they are normally stored. There have been times that, just after the storeroom is put back in order and as soon as the door is closed, the noise begins anew, and the items are again moved around.

Another report from the café is that of the hot dog and hamburger buns falling off of the shelves for no discernable reason. There are times when the chef will be grilling up a burger or hot dog, and the buns will plop down onto the back of the grill. What makes this more unusual is the fact that the buns are stored on a shelf a few feet away from the cooking area. It is almost as if the packages are being tossed at the chef—or at least the grill.

There were times during the town's mining days when contagious diseases would spread through Calico like water through a wash. Diphtheria, typhoid and others took a gruesome toll on the population and especially the very old and the young. As such, many children perished during these times. As a way to help the other children get through these rough times of seeing their classmates and friends pass, memorials just for the children would take place as a way for those left behind to say goodbye. These memorials would usually take place on the eastern side of the bridge—close enough to the school for an easy trek and far enough away that the kids shouldn't associate school with the tragedies. There have been numerous reports from employees and guests alike who have not only heard the sound of children in this area, but one of the employees from the Old Miners Café said they actually saw one of the wayward waifs staring out the window of the small shack that one of Calico's popcorn carts is attached to.

THE POPCORN CARTS

Calico has two popcorn carts—or wagons—along Main Street. The first cart is situated between the Rock and Fossil Shop and the blacksmith building. The other is located at the top of the street, across from the Sweet Shop and next to the bridge that leads over to the Old Miners Café. The popcorn cart is directly in front of a small shack under its shady overhang. The shack itself is unassuming, but those who have worked at the cart in the past have had a few interesting paranormal happenings occur.

Employees have heard children playing near the popcorn cart. The sound seemed to be coming from directly in front of them, even though there was no one in sight. This area is right where the children would have gathered when they were holding memorials for the kids who had passed from disease or an accident. This phenomenon has been reported quite often over the years and has become part of the legend surrounding Calico.

Children have not only been heard in this area; one of the employees at the Old Miner's Café may have actually seen one of the waifs one evening as she was closing up for the day. While picking up and washing down the outside tables that faced Main Street, the employee glanced toward the shack that is just across the bridge from the café. Having seen this view hundreds of times, she quickly turned away, but something caught her eye that didn't seem normal, and she turned back to take another look. This time, she saw what looked like a child staring back at her through the shack's window.

The shack is always locked up because it is mainly used for storage, and the town doesn't want anyone getting in there and possibly getting hurt. As the employee stood there, looking at the figure, she saw a young boy who was swaying, and she became concerned that he may have been locked inside somehow. After contacting the person who had the keys to the shack and telling him that she would meet him at the door, she walked across the bridge but kept her eye on the window and the young boy until she arrived at the front door to the shack. The employee with the keys was already waiting

It was in this window that an employee from the Old Miner's Café saw the spirit of "Chris" in the widow. The popcorn cart where spectral children can be heard is just visible to the right.

for her, and they hurriedly unlocked the door and walked inside together. The room was partially filled with stored items, but there was no sign of the boy anywhere. The windows didn't open, none were broken and there was no other way in or out of the shack except for the one door that they had entered through. Neither of the employees could explain where the child had gone, but both of them had worked at Calico long enough to know that unexplained things like this could happen in the town. After all, they did work at a place they knew to be haunted. This boy has been seen a few times since, even in the café often enough that those who work the area have given him the name Chris.

The other popcorn stand, which is a bit farther down Main Street, experiences so much paranormal activity that it has become the one place where no one wants to be assigned. So many employees complain about working there that it has become the place where all of the new hires are scheduled to work. So much goes on in this spot that many of the new hires have actually quit so they won't have to go back to work there.

Singing is often heard there, along with other strange sounds that can't be identified. The popcorn maker has been known to turn itself on for no reason; this has been a problem when employees have been away from the cart using the restroom, as the popcorn will burn if left unattended. Many times, employees have come back to a smoke-filled shop and have had to air it out while cleaning the popper and trying to serve guests. Cups will also mysteriously fall off the shelves, even though they are securely in place. Candy has been tossed about behind employees' backs, and in at least one extreme event, an employee said that, as she watched, the cups near the soda fountain rose up into the air, floated toward her and suddenly scattered in all directions, as if they had been thrown by an unseen hand.

No one has ever actually seen a spirit at the popcorn cart, nor has any ghost ever made its name clear. One can only speculate that it is a spirit that either enjoys playing jokes on the living or is so mad that a popcorn cart is in this location that it believes its antics will drive away the offending snack wagon. One thing seems clear, however: whatever the case may be, the spirit wishes to remain anonymous.

The Sweet Shop

Nothing is better on a hot day in the Mojave Desert than a cold drink—or better yet, a giant scoop of delicious ice cream. It gets very hot in Calico during the summer months. Because of this, the Sweet Shop gets so much business that a line forms outside the door. People will wait to buy ice-cold sodas, giant scoops of ice cream and some of the scrumptious fudge and other candies that the store offers. But most of those who wait in line will never know that the Sweet Shop is home to at least one ghost.

A ghost walk tour guide who also worked at Dorsey's Dog House next door to the Sweet Shop was once standing out on the front landing when she noticed a young boy running up the street as fast as he could go. As she followed his progress, she noticed that it looked like he was running from somebody. She didn't notice anyone following him but couldn't shake the idea that he was trying to get away from something. As she watched, the boy darted up the stairs and into the Sweet Shop. Wondering if something was wrong, the employee went over to the other store and asked the girl working there if she had seen a boy run in. The girl said she had and that the boy had run into the back room. The tour guide explained how the boy looked while running up the street, so they decided to check on him to make sure he was okay. As they entered the back room, they found that the child was not

The Calico Sweet Shop is said to have a mischievous young spirit by the name of Johnny.

there. The window in the back room was not able to be opened, there was no door other than the one they had come through and there was no way the boy could have hid or slipped past the store clerk without her seeing him. They looked around the rest of the shop, but there was no sign of the child anywhere. The two women just shook their heads and forgot about the event over the next few days.

A couple of days after the boy was seen running into the Sweet Shop, it happened a second time. The same child ran in, darted to the back of the store and disappeared. The clerk once again looked but found no one in the back room, and this time, she made sure that there was absolutely no way the boy could have gotten past her and back out the front door. Three more times, the boy was seen running into the store. The clerk and a couple of other employees decided that they would lay a trap for the child. Over the next few days, another employee would wait in the back room to catch the child and put an end to the mischief. On the second day, the trap was laid; a man was sitting in the back room, trying not to nod off, when he heard the clerk out front call out, "Did you get him?" Confused, the man left the back room to find out what the clerk meant. When he asked his fellow employee what she had said, he was told that the boy had just run into the store and disappeared into the back room. The man asked if she was sure that she had seen him come in, and in exasperation, she told him she was positive that she had clearly seen the boy duck into the back room. When her coworker told her that no one had come into where he was waiting and that he was sure he would have seen the child, they both realized that they had most likely been trying to catch a ghost.

This child has been seen quite often since his first appearance, and those who have seen him most frequently have given him the name Johnny. The boy is still seen from time to time, running down the street and into the Sweet Shop, but he is now also seen casually wandering around town. It also appears that Johnny has a sense of humor, as he likes to play jokes on the employees of the Sweet Shop. Some of the employees have reported entering the shop in the morning to find little handprints covering the display cases. Other times, clerks' phones will randomly ring when no one is calling, and random texts will be sent from their phones that are just a jumble of emoji's, symbols and nonsense words spread out over long lines of text. Johnny will also sometimes open the packaged popcorn bags and leave cryptic trails of popcorn through the shop for the clerks to find in the morning.

Johnny even rearranged a bunch of teddy bears that were being used as a fundraiser throughout the town in a very unusual way. Most of the stores in Calico had stocked the same distinct teddy bears, which were being sold to benefit a charitable organization. The bears at the Sweet Shop had been placed up on a high shelf behind the counter so that they were visible to any guests who came into the shop. One morning, as the clerk came into the store, she found that all of the teddy bears had been laid down; each bear had its head, face up, in the lap of the bear in front of it. The clerk had been the one who had closed the store the previous evening and knew that the bears had been placed properly when she had left for the night. The only other person with keys to the shop was the manager, who had been at another store in town when the clerk had left. The clerk also knew that it was not her manager's style to play a joke on her. The manager confirmed that it wasn't her. It is believed that Johnny may have been reacting to another employee trying to "catch" him in the store.

It seems that a few nights before Johnny's joke, another one of the clerks had spread flour over the floor, hoping to gain proof that Johnny existed. The following morning, the employee had his proof, as there were quite a few small footprints around the store in the flour. It may be that, after all the time that Johnny had been going into the store and running around town, he may not have liked that the other clerk was still trying to prove that he was actually there. It is said that Johnny still comes around the Sweet Shop on occasion. Who could blame him? What child wouldn't want to spend his time in the afterlife around candy, soda, fudge and ice cream?

CALICO HOUSE RESTAURANT

The Calico House is not one of the original buildings of Calico. Walter Knott built it to be exactly what it is: the only sit-down, indoor restaurant at Calico. There, you can find home-style cooking, including steak and eggs, omelets, pancakes and biscuits and gravy for breakfast; scrumptious sandwiches, burgers and soups and salads for lunch; and tri-tip, ham steaks with all of the trimmings and shepherd's pie for dinner. It is all served in a traditional western atmosphere, with hospitality and maybe even a ghost or two.

Employees at the Calico House Restaurant have said that, as they are getting ready to open in the morning, preparing food in the back kitchen area, they will hear the front doors open and guests call out to ask if there is anyone there and if the restaurant is open for business. But the staff never unlocks the doors until everything is ready for the guests. When one or more of the employees goes out to answer the people calling out to them, they find that the door is indeed locked and that no one is in the restaurant. Once the restaurant is open, the employees are allowed to keep the radio on as long as the music isn't too loud and is appropriate for all ages. All of the employees who were willing to tell their stories said that they have been busy with guests, taking orders or serving, when the radio's volume has suddenly been turned up to full blast. As the inside of the Calico House is quite spacious, the sound carries very well, and it can be hard to hear the person next to you if you aren't yelling, so the employees would all scramble to turn the volume back down. Many times, as the employees went about their business, the radio would again mysteriously return to full volume, sending the employees back into a mad scramble to lower the sound. One employee said that if you ask whoever is doing it to stop, they will cease doing it but only for a short time. In his book, Bill Cook says that there is a closet downstairs in the employee area that has a "thickness of the air" that many employees have mentioned, and he said that his wife and sister in-law have felt this thickness.

One employee told us that she was working one afternoon when a guest came in asking how to get up on the balcony. He wanted to get a couple of pictures of Wall Street Canyon from a higher vantage point. When the employee told the man that there was no way up to the balcony, he told her that he had just seen one of the street performers up there. Again, she told the guest that the balcony was just a façade and that there was no way up. The man again said that he had just seen someone there and that if it was just for town employees, he would be very careful not to let anyone know she he had let him up there. Once again, the girl said that there was no second floor in the building, no stairs to the balcony and no way to get up to it at all. The man finally left, mumbling something about her lying to him. However, the employee was telling the truth. The balcony is just for looks; there's no egress to it.

The ghosts are not confined to the interior of the Calico House Restaurant, as the tale above implies. While taking the ghost walk in Calico, the authors of this book were told that one of the rocking chairs, the third from the right-hand side on the front porch, had a tendency to rock on its own. It is said that, even when that one chair is in motion, all of the other rocking chairs on the porch remain still. People on the walks have even claimed that they have approached the chair as it was rocking, and as they got close, the chair suddenly stopped dead. Then, as they walked back to the tour group, the chair just as suddenly started rocking anew.

The Calico House Restaurant is the oldest established eatery in the town. It also has its fair share of apparitions.

As one guest noted above, there have been numerous reports of a cowboy slowly pacing the length of the restaurant's balcony. This apparition is seen so frequently that the employees of the Calico House have become accustomed to the questions that constantly come from guests who want to know who the man is or how to get up to the balcony themselves. As noted, this building is not original and was constructed without an actual second floor or stairway. There is also no record of a two-story structure ever occupying this location. One can only guess who this spectral cowboy is or why he has taken a fancy to the restaurant.

Other frequently reported phenomenon—and much more worrisome—are the reports of shadow figures lurking around the Calico House Restaurant. No one knows exactly what shadow figures are—ghosts, demons, extraterrestrial beings or time-traveling historians. What seems to be common among reports of these entities is that they are not usually friendly. These shadows have been seen walking along the balcony of the restaurant, going from one side to the other, seemingly without reason. As with the ghostly cowboy, no one is sure how the shadow people get up to the balcony, but as these figures have been seen in other odd places, it is believed that they can just appear wherever they like. It is odd, however, that they just pace back and forth along the walkway. These same figures have also been spotted walking along the front porch. They act similarly to their counterparts above, with the exception that they will sometimes wander into Main Street. Again, no one knows what their purpose is for walking along the balcony and porch of a building that was built for human gatherings, but someday, we may just find out.

Dining at the Calico House Restaurant is a must when visiting Calico; the food is delicious, the staff is welcoming and the atmosphere, with its spirited inhabitants, screams Wild West.

DORSEY'S DOG HOUSE

This little shop next door to the Sweet Shop may not be an eatery like the other locations in this chapter, but it does prove the fact that almost anything can be found in the ghost town. Named after perhaps the most famous local in Calico, Dorsey's Dog House caters to the flavors and nutrition of our four-legged friends. It also seems to have at least one spirit that employees know about. No one is really sure who or what the ghost is, and it has only been seen a couple of times, but when the spirit has been noticed, there is usually more than one witness to the phenomenon.

The first time this apparent apparition was seen was a few years ago, when one of the clerks who was working at Dorsey's was standing outside the store talking to a guest about the shop's wares. As they chatted, the employee glanced up, toward the little side door, and as she watched, something detached itself from one of the poles that holds up the patio cover. The clerk had worked at Calico for some years and was also a ghost walk tour guide for the town, so she was familiar with the ghosts that inhabit the town. This particular spirit was different, however, as it separated itself from the pole and retained the shape of the post. As she watched, this post-shaped apparition darted from the pole and went straight through the side door of Dorsey's Dog House.

Surprised, the clerk asked the guest she had been talking to if they had seen the same thing, and when the customer nodded, they looked at each other, grinned and hurried into the shop themselves. Unfortunately, by the time they entered the store, there was nothing to be found. The guest looked around the common area of Dorsey's while the employee searched the back of the shop, but neither found anything out of sorts or unusual. The two

A strange pole-like spirit has been seen at this doggie diner.

were both certain that they had seen something, and when the clerk told the guest about the town spirits, they both agreed that they had most likely seen some sort of ghost.

The employee said that, because Dorsey's is right next door to where the spirit of Johnny likes to play, what they saw may have in fact been Johnny playing a joke on her and the customer. The odd thing, however, is that every time Johnny has been seen running down the street and into the other shop, it is obvious that he is a little boy. This spirit looked nothing like a human at all. But whatever the spirit may have been—whether it was Johnny, another ghost or spirit or the pole itself—it has only been seen a couple of times. Hopefully, we will someday discover what the spirit is.

12

GHOSTS OF THE MAGGIE MINE

C alico was, is and always will be a mining town. Regardless of how it's been remade into a tourist experience and no matter how many buildings have been made souvenir shops, snack stands and craft studios, Calico will always be surrounded by deadly drops into catacombs that could spell doom for the unwary. Mine openings are scattered across the landscape like dandelions in a spring breeze. These were once the lifeblood of the town and those who lived and worked there. There are only two mines left in Calico that have been deemed safe for the general public to go spelunking in. The Silver King Mine—although it is not completely safe due to its steep ladders, narrow passageways and cramped corridors—is safe enough for tour groups led by experienced guides. Explorers must sign waivers stating they are in good health and that they acknowledge the dangers and release the tour company from liability. Even with all of this, many adventurers still sign up for this extreme tour of the dark Silver King Mine.

Some of these adventure seekers have come back with strange tales of shadows that followed their movements, the sounds of miners still at work and whispered conversations of people who weren't there. Those who know the legends of the Tommy Knockers wonder if these disturbances are the strange little gnomes still at work in the mines, and others believe that they are the ghosts of miners who died in the mines and are unable to find rest in the afterlife. Regardless of the truth behind these tales, the reports from the Silver King are nothing compared to stories that come from the more widely traveled Maggie Mine directly in the heart of the town of Calico.

Although it is not an original building, the structure leading into the infamous Maggie Mine is a museum in its own right.

The Maggie Mine is so safe that a mere three-dollar admission fee is all it takes to enter this historic and quite haunted silver mine. On entering the adit of the mine, one will notice that, unlike most mines, there are no support timbers lining the passageways or walls. The reason for this is that the Maggie Mine was bored from ancient volcanic ash that had hardened into stone, making the need for support almost nonexistent. It was much easier for miners to blast out the rock and begin the mining process rather than go through the tedious procedure of shoring that was required for most mining operations. This also makes the Maggie Mine the perfect museum, where tourists can learn and explore a real silver mine.

The mine was begun in 1882, the same year Maurice Mulcahy died in a mining accident in Nevada. Maurice's widow, Catherine, moved the family to Calico a year later. Sons, John, Maurice Jr. and Jim followed in their father's footsteps and began mining in the Calico Hills. It was around 1916 that John Mulcahy purchased the mine and renamed it Maggie Mine. The story says that the name was inspired by a song that was very popular at the time. Unfortunately, this cannot be verified, but it has become the adopted tale. Whatever the reason, the Mulcahys worked this mine for over twenty years. Another tale regarding the Mulcahys says that the brothers actually lived in the mine itself. How this tale came to pass has been lost to history, but the truth of the matter is that the brothers lived in houses in the town of Calico. The area in the mine that is said to have been their living space was used by the Mulcahys but not as their home. There were times that they worked long hours and napped in the mine instead of making the trek home. Other times, they used the area to sleep off a long night at one of the saloons instead of facing the wrath of their significant others.

John Mulcahy died in 1931, working the mine right up to his death. Maurice would continue on until 1942, when he himself passed. Not much is known about their brother Jim, but we know that he also worked in the mine for many years. Quite a few Mulcahy family members are buried in the Daggett Cemetery, and the name Mulcahy has become as synonymous with Calico as the name King. It is said that, in total, the Maggie Mine produced $65,000 in silver ore. Today, the mine is nothing more than a tourist exhibit. Approximately one thousand feet of the mine is open for guests to explore. It is perhaps one of the finest examples of a mine that one can safely traverse in order to see just what miners had to endure during their long, tedious workdays buried deep in the darkness of Mother Earth. When Walter Knott bought the town of Calico and ventured into the Maggie Mine for the first time, he would have seen mine cart tracks winding down the center of the mine shafts. These tracks were quickly removed, but they gave Knott the inspiration for the Mine Train Ride that still takes amusement park guests around a fictional Maggie Mine at the world-famous Knott's Berry Farm in Buena Park, California, today. The Maggie Mine is not only an important piece of state mining history, it is also one of the most haunted places in Calico Ghost Town.

One of the strangest tales from the mine comes from a former employee. The woman said that, one day, as she was getting ready to let a couple of guests into the mine, she was just about to open one of the double doors when a pipe fell from the ceiling and almost hit her. It wasn't a large pipe, but if it had struck her, it would have given her a nice bump on the head— or worse. She looked up to where the pipe had seemingly fallen from and found that there were no other pipes above her. Not only was there no sign of where the pipe could have fallen from, there was no place where a pipe could have been placed in the ceiling. There were no indents, no hangers and no holes where the pipe could have been fitted. After speaking with the owners, they confirmed that there were no pipes anywhere in any of the ceilings inside the mine. To this day, neither the owners nor the employee have been able to figure out how that pipe almost hit her.

Looking back toward the entrance from deep inside the Maggie Mine.

This same employee tells the story of a film crew that was getting ready for a shoot when the cameraman entered the mine to look for shooting locations. He had only been in the mine for about five minutes when he came running out as fast as he could. After the man calmed down enough to speak, he said that, as he neared the fork in the passageway, he heard what sounded like miners at work. He went on to say that, as disturbing as this was, he continued down the shaft, and when he got to the fork itself, he felt someone lightly push him, as if they were trying to get him out of the way. He turned to look, and there was nobody there. He knew he was the only one in the mine at the time, and when he felt someone touch him again, he bolted for the exit. The cameraman didn't go back into the mine again.

The fork in the Maggie Mine has been an area of high activity. Reports have come in so often from guests that many who work there believe that the fork may be the most haunted part of the mine. Most of the claims have been about orbs caught on camera. As most paranormal investigators know, orbs are one of the most controversial phenomena in the community. Orbs can be anything from dust to bugs flying around in the dark. That being said, there have been many reports of balls of light, which can be seen with the naked eye, seemingly flying around those present, and they have

Darkness awaits all who dare to enter.

reportedly actually followed guests as they toured the mine. These balls of light, coupled with the massive amount of orb activity, are enough to make one wonder about the area.

Another part of the mine where orbs are frequently seen is the Glory Hole. This section of the mine is where the largest vein of ore was discovered, and as such, it had the largest work force employed. Orbs are not the only strange things experienced here. Guests touring the Maggie Mine have come out asking if the mine has speakers piping in the sounds of men working the ore in the Glory Hole. There are no such speakers, but many of the guests swear that they heard the sound of men working, hammers "tinking" away at the stone and miners talking and that they saw shadows darting around behind the wire fencing that now blocks the access point to the Glory Hole itself.

Across the passageway, very near the Glory Hole, is the room where the Mulcahy brothers would take their naps, sleep off their drunkenness and take their meals while working their claim. This area was, in effect, the

Mulcahy's campsite. Reports from this area range from hearing what sounds like a stove being ignited to actually seeing figures sleeping in the cots. The tour operators do have mannequins in this room, so the sight of a sleeping figure can be easily dismissed—that is, unless snoring can be heard in the small room, as has happened on occasion. The sound of a lighter has also been heard there, which makes one wonder if the Mulcahys have found the joys in modern stove and lamp lighting.

Dead Man's Drift is said to also have quite a bit of ghostly activity, and reports from this section of the mine are very common. Dead Man's Drift is the area near the mine's stope; this is where a group of veins came together, and a series of steps were created so that the ore could be raised to the top of the mountain or hill. These stopes became necessary when the distance to haul the ore out of the mine adit became greater than just lifting it out through the top of the hill. Oftentimes, the ore would be lifted using buckets raised by small, motorized winches. The stope in the Maggie Mine is considered an area of high activity. This section of the mine is now gated off due to the fact that the steps have become unstable for the amount of foot traffic that runs through the mine. Guests are still allowed to peer through the wire gate, and many have reported seeing shadows just inside the closed off area. People have often heard the sound of women talking and giggling as they pass by. It was considered to bring extreme bad luck if women entered a mine, especially if they had red hair, so it is very odd that reports of this nature are so frequently heard. At times, with waivers signed, the gate to the drift is opened for groups to perform paranormal investigations in the area. During one of these investigations, a group was conducting an EVP session when a member of the group, who was standing very near a precipice, was forcefully pushed by unseen hands. Luckily, another group member was nearby and managed to catch the other team member before they were harmed.

In his book *Ghostly Guide to Calico Ghost Town*, Bill Cook tells a story of a family that had an interesting encounter in the mine. Bill said that, when he owned the Old-Time Photo Studio on Main Street, a family came in one day after they had just left the Maggie Mine. The mother of a five-year-old girl was upset at her daughter because she kept talking about people who weren't there while they were in the mine. The mother told Bill and his wife how the little girl kept trying to get them to move aside for men as they passed by at the "Y" in the mine. The girl's parents couldn't see anybody, but the little girl insisted that the miners needed to pass them so that they could continue with their work. Many people believe that children can more

The exit from the Maggie Mine is next to another of the mine's dangerous shafts. Could this be where the reported spirits walking down the staircase emanate from?

easily see things that we, as adults, cannot. This may be a case in which the woman's daughter was more attuned to the spirits of the mine and could see the ghostly miners, while her parents could not.

Perhaps the most haunted section of the Maggie Mine is the area where one must climb a staircase to exit through the back of the mine when they are done exploring its passageways. Although the stairway is not original to the mine, many people claim to see miners descending down the long, dark steps, as if they are arriving for work. This exit was not there while the mine was operational, so it is unclear why these spectral miners would be walking down the stairway. Maybe they just find it to be an easier egress than going in through the adit. Some of the reports from folks who have seen these apparitions say that many of the spirits appear to be in various states of decay. One gentleman even claimed that, at first, he thought they were Halloween projections to make guests think they were being attacked by a hoard of zombies.

Another lady mentioned that she was touring the mine with her blind grandmother. As she walked through the mine, she held her grandmother's hand to direct her. The woman thought it was odd that, as they neared the stairway, her grandmother began swatting at her hand, saying, "Tell them to stop." She asked her grandmother who she was talking about, and the older woman said, "The men who keep holding my hand." The woman told her grandmother that no one else was holding her hand, but the woman just said, "No, my other hand." They continued to walk, and the older woman began swatting her free hand, asking those she thought were holding it to let go. Finally, as they were about to walk up the exit, the grandmother demanded the men leave her alone, and they stopped trying to grab her hand. It is unclear why the spirits were so concerned with the elderly woman, but some employees believe that they were trying to make sure she was taken care of as she walked through their territory. Others believe that it may have been the Tommy Knockers and that they were, for the same reasons, looking after the grandmother.

The building and gift shop at the front of the Maggie Mine is, of course, not original, but inside, one can find various mining objects, including a few small rock crushers, a giant ore bucket and other rare mining artifacts; there is even an old dry washer one can marvel at. All of these objects are located

From this stairway exit, ghastly images of ghosts have been reported frequently.

in a safe and comfortable environment, which can't be found at any other mine that the public is allowed to explore. The one thing that many people are unaware of is that the Maggie Mine may also show its guests some true mining spirit. So, as you wander through the dark passages and peer into the dark recesses of this mining time capsule, remember, it may not be one of the mannequins you are looking at; it may be one of the former miners or maybe even one of the elusive Tommy Knockers.

13.

AMUSEMENTS AND OTHER POLTERGEISTS OF INTEREST

There are many things to do in Calico Ghost Town. Touring the Maggie Mine is a wonderful way to step back into the shoes of the miners who made the town what it was and what it is today. The town's many shops can keep you busy for hours on end, and the many eateries in the town will most assuredly satisfy your appetite. But Calico is much more than just a tourist town where you can shop and eat. It is a piece of history where you can learn and see what life was like in California during its mining days. As such, there are still parts of that history that can be explored today. Some may only look at the town in wonder; others may step inside to see how the citizens of Calico lived, and others still, thanks to Walter Knott, can ride along to see the mining district in all its glory.

CALICO PARK OFFICE

This building is the second on your left as you enter the town. It is the oldest existing wooden structure in Calico. At one time, there were three of these small buildings on this lot. Together, they made up the "red-light" district of the town, serving miners twenty-four hours a day, seven days a week. Although this area wasn't talked about much, it was as popular—if not more so—than the many saloons that dotted Calico at the time. Today, the building has been repurposed and is used as the office space for the rangers and employees who see to the town's care and maintenance. Claims from

The park office is one of the red-light district's original buildings.

this area only seem to come in during the evening hours, when the town is shutting down from the day's activities. As with the bridge that leads to the Old Miners Café, the scent of rosewater and lavender is often smelled by those nearby, along with the muffled sounds of girls quietly chatting or giggling at jokes that only they can hear. These sounds and smells are very common near the building, and where the other structures once stood.

There is one disturbing report that keeps coming up regarding a black figure that is seen standing just inside the front-right window of the office. No one has figured out who or what the apparition might be, but those who have seen the figure have said that it will stare out at those watching as if it is as interested in them as they are in it. The entity has been seen on the front porch, but once it is seen, it immediately disappears into the building, only to reappear looking out the window. It has not been determined whether the figure is a male or a female, but since the building was once part of a brothel, it is assumed that it is most likely one of the many prostitutes who once occupied and worked in the industry. This theory seems to be borne out of the fact that the same lavender and rosewater scents have been smelled at the same times the figure has been seen. If it is one of the former "ladies of the evening," it is unclear why she seems to be dressed all in black, as if she's wearing a mourning gown. Hopefully, we will someday come to learn who or what this figure may actually be.

APPLEWHITE LIVERY

There is a large empty lot part way up Main Street; it is located on the left and is surrounded by a wooden corral. This area was originally the site of the Applewhite Livery Barn, which was across the street from the Applewhite Boardinghouse. The barn was large enough to hold crowds of people, so it became a gathering place for the townsfolk; it was where they held Christmas gatherings, church services and, quite often, town dances. The barn burned down in the fire of 1887 and was never rebuilt. Other buildings sprang up on the site over time, including, it is said, a town hall. All of these other structures were destroyed by fires, earthquakes and time, but the property itself seems to only remember the good times, when it was home to a social hall.

Over the years, it has been common for employees and guests alike to hear music coming from the area inside the corral. Even when there are no events taking place at Calico, when there are no bands set up to amuse the tourists, music has been heard seemingly coming from thin air. There are other times that the music has been accompanied by the sound of a happy crowd in the same area. Since this was a place of fun and enjoyment, where the whole town was invited, could this be a residual from those days of happiness? Or maybe it is the townsfolk gathering in the afterlife to enjoy each other's company.

In Bill Cooks book, he says that, one evening, after closing up the Calico Woodworking Shop he owned at the time, he and his wife, Jill, were relaxing on the front porch, listening to authentic 1880s music, when his wife suddenly asked him if he heard the sound of a crowd. After she mentioned it, Bill himself heard the gathering, and it sounded as if it was coming from the lot next to their shop. Bill got up and walked toward the lot that was right next to their store, and as he got closer, the sound got louder. He said that, when he finally looked into the lot itself, the noise suddenly ceased.

Calico is known for holding large events for tourists; its Civil War Days, Old Calico Days and others are held annually, and they need actors and reenactors to make the shows possible. During some of these events, the large lot is sometimes used for the participant's RVs and trailers so that they don't have to spend money on hotels or other lodging. One year, while a participating couple had their trailer parked in the corral, they heard a dog barking outside. The woman looked up from cooking and noticed a dark figure standing out in front of their RV. Wanting to make sure everything was OK, the woman asked her husband to go out and check who it was. Her

It was here that a reenactor and his wife saw the apparition of what they believed to be a suicide victim.

husband went outside and saw a man sitting on a bench they had in front of their trailer. He asked the man if he needed something, and when he received no response, he told the figure that he couldn't stay there and that he needed to move on. The figure on the bench turned his head toward the man, but before he could turn to look at him, the figure vanished. After the man went back in to tell his wife what had happened, she immediately made her husband pack up and leave. To this day, the reenactors still participate but refuse to stay in town.

Many people have seen a lone figure of a man walking across the street, toward the now-empty lot. This shadowy figure has been seen coming from where the old Applewhite Boardinghouse used to be; on occasion, he has been seen coming from the direction of the Calico House Restaurant. (This figure should not be confused with the other shadow figure that is seen coming from the restaurant.) Many people believe that this spirit may belong to Mr. J.I. Spainhour, who shot himself while staying in the boardinghouse in 1884; he is now buried in the Calico Cemetery. Could this be the same gentleman that the reenactor saw sitting on his bench?

Most people don't think about vacant lots being haunted, but when a spirit or spirits become attached to a place where a building once stood, who is to say what their reality may be? So, if you are walking past this empty corral and hear music or a crowd, look around and see whether the town is entertaining you or if the spirits are entertaining themselves.

Calico Firehouse

On the right side of the street, near the Lane House Museum, sits the Calico Firehouse. During the life of the town, even into modern times fire has been the bane of Calico. When the fire raged through the town in the early days it was up to the townsfolk to man buckets full of water to try and douse the flames destroying their town. As time progressed, crude apparatus was created so the populace could be safe while allowing trained firefighters to man pumps and hoses to extinguish the blazes. The technology improved with time and today things are much better than they were in the days when whole towns would be lost to the ravages of flame. Through it all, from the beginnings of man's need to save their belongings up to the modern age, one thing has remained constant…the fire bell.

Today, the firehouse in Calico is a small museum with an old 1800s fire wagon inside that teaches guests what it must have been like to fight fires in the hot desert climate in a town made of wood. The firehouse is still there and its warning bell still sits within its tower awaiting a hand to pull its string and alert the town of impending hardship. Unfortunately, even if a rope was pulled the bell still wouldn't sound. This is because the elements and time have frozen the bell in place with rust. The bell couldn't ring if it wanted to…or could it?

It still amazes those working at Calico and those in the know that at various times, and for seemingly no reason a bell will be heard throughout town. When the bell is heard, the towns folk know that they are hearing the bell atop the old firehouse. Guests have asked if the bell is added for character

Even though this fire bell is so rusted that it can no longer move, there are times it will still ring out.

and others marvel at the acoustics of the sound as they look up and realize the bell isn't moving and the sound must be coming from a speaker set high above them. It isn't, of course, and there is no speaker. One can only wonder if this phantom bell rings as a reminder of what can and has happened at Calico when man forgets that nature rules and not they themselves?

HANK'S HOTEL

Hank's Hotel is not an original structure from Calico's days as a mining town. Walter Knott built the structure as a way to add original color to the town and to give those working at the town a place to stay. Over the years, Hank's has been used as a temporary lodging for employees, as a meeting place for the employees of the town and as an artist's colony. There has been one thing it has been used for that hasn't changed in all of the years Hank's Hotel has been in existence: a residence for ghosts.

When the hotel was used as a gathering place for meetings, employees would hear loud bangs coming from upstairs, and oftentimes, their

Hank's Hotel is not original to Calico, but that has not stopped the spirits from "renting" out the rooms.

meetings would be disrupted by the lights switching on and off at random times. Those who used Hank's as a temporary home would often find that their belongings had been moved around and misplaced, and they found items in their rooms that didn't belong to them. Shadow figures have been seen wandering around outside the building, and people have reported seeing these same figures passing by the windows inside the hotel. There have also been reports of a well-dressed couple standing on the balcony just above the entrance to the hotel. The couple appears to be in late-1800s attire.

A warning for men: There is a female spirit that has been seen quite often at the junction of Main Street, where it turns to go down to Hank's Hotel. The lady seems to beckon the men to follow her to Hank's—or at least to follow her in that direction—for unknown reasons. No one has followed this female spirit—that we know of anyway—so if you happen to see her and decide to follow, please tell us what she is after if you make it back.

At one time, the building was used as an artist's studio, where painters, potters, sculptors and the like could come, set up and consult their muse. Once, as an artist was just finishing up for the day, she stood back, took one more look at the oil painting she was working on, carefully flipped the protective cover over, locked her studio and the hotel and went home for the day. The following morning, when she arrived back at Hank's, she went upstairs to her studio, unlocked the door and looked over to her painting to see how it was drying. What she found was a ruined canvas. Someone had turned up her cover, exposed the wet paint and left handprints streaking down through the artwork. Neither she nor the rangers who came to investigate could find any type of forced entry; there were no wet handprints, footprints or other telltale signs that anyone had been in the building overnight. It appeared to just be another case of the spirits at Hank's Hotel making themselves known. It also proves the old adage that everyone is a critic—even ghosts, it would seem.

Calico Town Hall

Although this is not the original town hall for Calico, this building started out as the Calico Artisan, an art studio for those who left Hank's Hotel and needed a place to sell their works. Today, the town hall still has artwork inside, but there is no one there to sell—it is just a place to look at the marvelous creations. Well, to say no one is there may not be completely accurate, as the building does have its share of spirits.

When it was being used as an art studio, many of the artists would get the feeling that they were being watched, and some got the feeling that the spirit was standing right behind them, looking over their shoulder. For those artists who left Hank's due to its spirit activity, this was the last straw for them, and many left the town for good. After the building became a town hall and showcase gallery, reports of spirit activity didn't diminish, but the type of activity changed. One report came from a cleaning crew who was getting the building ready for an event. As they were cleaning, the front-right door slammed shut. This, in and of itself, didn't alarm them, so one of them opened the door, placed the metal bar back into the hole in the floor to keep it open and went back to work. Once again, the door slammed shut. This time, they knew that it wasn't the wind or any other random cause because they both clearly heard the bolt being moved just before the door closed.

Another incident took place one day when a tour guide was talking to a woman whose likeness was hanging on the wall. The woman and the guide heard three distinct knocks on the piano as they were chatting. The guide let out a little chuckle, walked over to the piano and knocked three times himself. When three more knocks sounded on the piano, they both decided it was time to leave. There have also been reports, albeit rare, of two figures standing just to the right of the front doors. The identity of the figures is unclear, and since they are not seen often, it may be a long time before we can figure out who these spirits may be.

The Bottle House

The Bottle House is another Knott creation. It is a scaled-down representation of the type of structures that can be found in other towns throughout the West. This structure is also a store, but since it is only open on certain weekends, it was decided to put it in this chapter. There is very little paranormal activity associated with this building, but there is one interesting tale.

It seems that a doll the store had placed behind the counter turned up missing one day when the shop had been closed up tight. No video could be found of anyone getting into the store, and all the footage showed was the doll sitting there one minute and disappearing the next. The doll wasn't an expensive item, but some of the employees had grown attached to him, so it was a minor loss to the store. The doll had been mostly forgotten—as lost merchandise usually is—when, two months after the doll had disappeared, it mysteriously showed up on a bench in front of the Mystery Shack. Again, video surveillance footage was examined, and as before, it showed no one

This is the doll that disappeared from the Bottle House and then mysteriously reappeared months later.

putting the doll on the bench. It wasn't there, and then, inexplicably, it appeared on the bench. The doll is now back where it belongs: at the Bottle House Shop. It is not for sale and has been given a name and a place of prominence. It now seems content to stay put.

THE MYSTERY SHACK

There were originally two Mystery Shacks: the one in Calico, and the other, which was called the Ghost Shack, in Calico Ghost Town in Knott's Berry Farm. The one at the amusement park was closed years ago. Fortunately, you can still explore the wonders of the optical illusions and sleight of sight misdirections at the Mystery Shack in the real Calico Ghost Town. If you are one of the lucky volunteers who is picked to participate in the fun, you might also get a little help from the friendly spirit who visits the attraction from time to time. Over the years, the Mystery Shack area has had a few minor reports of activity; orbs have been seen, strange lights have darted around and an old man, on occasion, has sat in the waiting area. Maybe it was this old timer or another spirit of the town who aided a guest in getting out of a particularly insidious optical illusion test.

The Mystery Shack uses deception in the form of geometry to fool the mind into thinking one thing while the opposite is actually reality (up is actually down, sideways is actually forward and other things of this nature). One of the illusions involves a chair that is seemingly straight up and down, but it is almost impossible for women to get out of, and it is even worse for men. During one of the tours, a man volunteered to sit in the chair, and he tried to stand up on his own. Of course, he was unable to, no matter how hard he tried. And from what the tour guides said, very few have ever tried quite as hard. Since the tour needed to move along, the guide moved to help the man up when, suddenly, the man jumped out of the chair as if he was pulled out of it. The entire group looked stunned, but none were more surprised than the man himself, who said he felt as if he had been yanked out of the chair. With the tour group shaking their heads, they moved along to the next mystery.

A few days after this tour, the Calico Mystery Shack received a photo from a person who had been on the tour that day. They had snapped the picture just as the man had leapt from the chair, and in the picture, very close to the man's shoulder, there is what appears to be hands pushing the man from the chair. Could there have been a spirit tagging along on the tour? Could this ghost have wanted the man to give up so that the tour would continue? No one is sure, but if you want to see the photo for yourself, sign up for the town ghost walk. You won't be disappointed.

THE DOLL HOUSE

This little cottage, which is set just off Main Street, along the path that leads to the Maggie Mine, was built to house a caretaker or another important employee of Calico. Perhaps the best known and certainly the most loved character to live in this house was Tumbleweed Harris. Now buried in the Calico Cemetery, Harris was a fixture in the town and served as the last marshal; he was also a street performer, greeter and all-around town color character. Tumbleweed was always willing to help out the other performers; he took many under his wing and became an uncle to many. Harris also loved children. It wasn't unusual to find the man sitting with a

Tumbleweed Harris lived here while working for Calico. It is said that he is still living in the Doll House, long after his death.

child, telling them stories about the Old West and Calico and bringing a smile to their faces, as well as their parents'. Tumbleweed Harris may have enjoyed it so much that, after his death, he may have decided to continue on in the afterlife.

There have been several inquiries at the town office about a man with a long, bushy white beard wearing a red long john shirt, jeans and suspenders who had been telling stories to their children. None of the parents ever actually saw the man, but they heard from their kids about what a great storyteller he was. They were asking because they wanted to thank him for making their children happy. The rangers, not really wanting anyone to know about the spirits in town, simply played dumb and told them they would pass on the compliment.

One of the stories told says that, one day, while spending a nice afternoon at Calico, a man was admiring the Doll House while his little girl played nearby. The father thought it was time to go and told his daughter, but she told him, "Not until the end of the story, Daddy." The man was a bit confused and asked her what she was talking about. The little girl pointed at an empty bench next to the Doll House and said, "Not until the nice man is finished telling me the story." The father again tried to get his daughter to leave, but she shushed him and turned back to the empty bench. His daughter seemed to be paying close attention to something, so he decided to watch her to see what she would do. After only a few more minutes, the girl smiled, waved and with a happy tone called out, "OK, bye, thank you!" She then turned to her dad, told him they could leave and started off down the wooden walkway.

The father had to hurry to catch up to the girl, but when he finally did, he pulled her to a stop and asked what that was all about. His daughter told him that the nice old man with the beard had been telling her stories about Calico while he admired the man's house. She said that he—the girl's father—had been right in the middle of a story that she was enjoying and that she didn't want to be rude to the nice old man. The father was surprised that his daughter would make up such a tale and asked her to describe the man. She told him he had a long white beard, a red shirt and blue pants with suspenders. She also told him that the man said thank you for stopping by his house for a visit. The girl then happily went on her way to explore other parts of Calico. This story is told quite often by other parents with differing plot points, but they are all alike, in that their children come away happy and with stories about Calico that they wouldn't know unless someone had told them. This interaction and kindness to children is just like something Tumbleweed would have done while he was alive.

Harris is not only seen near the Doll House. He is often spotted on a bench near the entrance to Calico, whittling away at a piece of wood. Another place where Tumbleweed is reported is near the old sheriff's office. This was also the marshal's office, and since Harris was the last town marshal, it shouldn't be hard to understand why he would hang around there. There are times at night that the rangers patrol the town to make sure all is well, and it is then that they hear the sound of boots walking along the boardwalks. They see no one when this occurs, and many of the rangers believe that this is Harris, still making sure the town he loved is safe and secure.

Harris passed away in 1979, and when he was laid to rest in the town cemetery, the crowd of townsfolk and employees in attendance was huge. For Harris, Calico had become his home, and both the town and those who worked and played there had become his family. It should be no surprise that Tumbleweed is still around, looking after things and teaching the children the history of Calico.

THE CALICO AND ODESSA RAILROAD

Not an original to the town of Calico, this ride was constructed in the 1960s and is still a popular attraction today. The train takes guests on a short excursion around the canyons and hills to see areas that are otherwise hard to reach. The whole trek takes about ten minutes and is a pleasant way to relax in the desert sun. Reports of ghostly activity on the ride are rare, but there have been a couple that are worth mentioning.

More than once, and usually in the evening, the train bell has been known to ring, even though the ride is shut down and no one is near the locomotive to sound it. The best chance one has to hear the train bell ringing is to participate in the town ghost walk, as this is held around the time the bell is usually heard.

Another tale comes from an employee at the Old-Time Photo Shop. The young lady said that a few years ago, she and a few friends went walking along the tracks after a Halloween event had shut down for the night. As they were walking along, they saw a man in western garb standing in the middle of the rails with his back to them. The man was silhouetted in the moonlight, and they assumed he was one of the town actors out for a stroll. As they neared him, the man turned toward them, stared at them for just a second and then vanished. The girl said that all they could see was that he was wearing a duster over his clothes and that he made them all feel uncomfortable. No one knows who this spirit is, but maybe he is the one who keeps ringing the bell.

THE SCHOOLHOUSE

This is another building that is not original to the town, but it is a scaled-down replica of the second Calico schoolhouse. It is also perhaps the most famous haunt in the town of Calico—this is because of one story that seems to repeat itself many times and from many diverse people. The event revolves around a former schoolteacher who is still trying to educate anyone who is willing to learn. What most people don't understand is that there is much more going on at the school than the haunts of this one lone spirit.

There is a story that has become so familiar to the rangers and employees at Calico that all they can do when someone reports it is smile at whoever

The Calico Schoolhouse is considered by many to be the most haunted building in Calico.

is doing the talking. People will come in asking about the character up at the school, who they had just talked to and who had explained all of the minute details of having to teach one class with so many different age groups in so many different grades and how it makes one want to pull their hair out. The guests come in marveling at the way the woman carried herself and how she was so knowledgeable about the era that it was almost as if she had lived it herself. The guests always want to compliment the young lady, and they want to make sure the town management appreciates her hard work. The rangers used to explain that there was no one working in the schoolhouse and that there was no young lady dressed as the teacher or anyone working in the town who had in-depth knowledge of what it was like to be an educator in the 1800s and early 1900s. Now, the staff just say thank you to the guests, and they tell them they will let the young woman know she was complimented. They no longer tell them that the woman they had just seen was a ghost.

No one is completely sure who the teacher is, but many believe she is Margaret Kincaid Olivier. Olivier was the last teacher in the town and was buried in the Calico Cemetery. The teacher also appeared to a couple from Europe and was gracious enough to pose for photos with them. According to

Inside this classroom, the ghosts of children have been seen and interacted with.

the couple, when they returned home and looked at their pictures, the staff member didn't appear in any of the shots.

Olivier isn't the only spirit making herself known at the schoolhouse. There is a little girl who is often seen peering out of the school's windows. This child will smile and wave at passersby who happen to catch her looking. Other children have been seen inside the classroom, sitting at their desks, while a teacher, not always Mrs. Olivier, directs lessons. Once, during a tour of the school, the kids who were participating were given chalkboards while they sat at the old desks. One of the children stood up, handed his board back and began walking toward the doors at the front. After setting the chalkboard down, the tour guide looked up, but the boy was nowhere to be found, and none of the parents were missing a child. Another manifestation at the school interacts with people who snap selfies in front of the school's windows. It is not uncommon for the guests to look down at their selfie and see someone looking back at them through the windows. The figure is usually that of one of the teachers, but on a few occasions, kids have been seen peeking back. There are other times that visitors can see someone standing in the picture, but the figure is too dark to make out.

LANE HOUSE

John and Lucy Lane lived in Calico longer than anyone else. The house they shared miraculously survived the many fires, as well as the ravages of the harsh desert climate. No longer set up as a home, the Lane House is now a museum that honors the Lanes and what they meant to the town of Calico. Lucy, it seems, may still call the museum home.

The Lane House is open for anyone who wants to look around. There are no docents stationed in the house to keep an eye on things—unless you count Lucy. Many people, while admiring the museum, have heard the sounds of footsteps when no one else was in the building, and others have reported hearing greetings called out to them from empty rooms. The voices are not always female, however. This could be because the building was actually the courthouse and post office before the Lanes took it over in the 1920s.

The belief that Lucy still resides in her old home comes from the many reports of people who have seen her walking across Main Street, from the Lanes' general store, usually carrying what looks like a bag of groceries, and into the Lane House. Even though Lucy is buried in the town of San Jacinto, California, it seems she still prefers her old stomping grounds of Calico.

Lucy Lane has been heard inside her old home.

BLACKSMITH SHOP

The blacksmith building was erected under the guidance of "Calico" Fred Noller; it was to be a true representation of an authentic blacksmith shop from the 1800s. The "smithy" is used in this capacity, with talented smiths performing their craft during events, reenactments and during Old Calico Days. The rest of the time, the forge and bellows are cold and quiet, waiting for the next spark to ignite their fires. However, they don't always wait for a live human to light that fire.

There have been many reports from guests who were walking by the blacksmith shop or looking into the darkened work area when they suddenly felt an intense heat. They say that it is almost as if the forge were lit, even though they can see it isn't. The heat is not always severe, but on occasion, it radiates just enough for guests to feel its warmth, almost as if the forge were cooling down from a day's work. Could the old smiths of Calico still be plying their trade in the afterlife? The phantom heat may give the answer.

This Black Maria may still contain one of its former "passengers."

People can still feel heat from the forge, long after it was extinguished.

Next to the blacksmith building, under an eave, there is an old horse-drawn hearse, a Black Maria. This hearse has been known to fog up on the inside for no reason, and once, as the owner of the ghost walk tour looked on, she saw what appeared to be a spectral hand trace down the steamed-up glass, as if someone was inside and wanted out. The Black Maria has been known to make people feel uncomfortable and ill at ease when looking at it. Could one of the old passengers still be catching a ride?

14.

A Paranormal Shopping Spree

There are very few, if any, buildings in Calico that do not have a ghost residing in them. Even the buildings that were constructed by Walter Knott when he rebuilt the town have ghosts that appear to have made these places home. The eateries, museums, curiosities and attractions are all said to be haunted. This includes the buildings that have been turned into souvenir shops, candle sellers, leather good shops and woodworks. All of them have tales of things that go *bump* in the aisles, of things that jump off the shelves and of employees who have become friendly acquaintances with the ghosts themselves. All of this activity could have another explanation; with many different items in many different shops, it could be that just a few ghosts are traveling to the various stores, moving along on their own paranormal shopping spree.

CALICO WOODWORKS

The Calico Woodworks sells handcrafted wood art, wall hangings and other fine wood crafts for the home. This shop is also known for carrying many period wooden puzzles, games, toys and just about anything else you didn't know you wanted. It is also home to a spirit that loves to sit and whittle away the time on the wooden bench out in front of the store. Many people believe this spirit to be Tumbleweed Harris, as he loved to shape things out of bits and pieces of wood he found. The spot where this spirit whiles away the time is also near the place where Harris acted as greeter for the town. It is known that Tumbleweed is still in Calico long after his death, so it would not be surprising to find him here, enjoying the sunshine. This is also the store that Bill Cook, the original ghost walk tour guide, owned, and it is where he and his wife heard what he called "old-timey" music coming from the empty lot next door, where the town gathering place once stood.

LANE'S GENERAL STORE

John and Lucy Lane opened this store in Calico in the late 1800s, and they ran it until there were so few people left in town and visitors only trickled in that it was no longer profitable. The store, which was an original building in the town, has gone through various iterations since the town was brought back to life by Walter Knott, but through it all, it has remained a fixture in the town of Calico—along with its ghosts.

There is a basement in this shop that was added by John Lane. He put the door to the basement in the front boardwalk because the back of the store butts up to the side of Wall Street Canyon. This basement is dark and creepy—at least, according to the employees. One story about the basement came from an employee who experienced something while they were busy stocking a shipment of goods that had come in. While he was busy placing things in order, the man began to get the uncomfortable feeling that he was being watched. No matter how hard he tried, he couldn't shake the feeling. He turned to where he felt the gaze was coming from, but he could never see anyone there. He tried to put it out of his mind, but he couldn't put the feeling behind him. He turned once more to where he felt he was being watched, and this time, when he looked, there was an old lady standing directly behind him, almost touching him. The guy let out a scream, left what he was doing and ran out. He never went into the basement alone ever again.

This ghost is thought to be Lucy Lane still keeping an eye on her store. As Lucy is seen quite often walking from the store to her house directly across the street, this is most likely the case. Her husband, John, may also be keeping an eye on the business that he and his wife so lovingly built. The employees at the store say they often see the figure of a man standing by the doorway. He appears to be wearing period clothing and is often seen smoking a cigar.

The Lanes may both be watching over their store. Lucy is often seen walking from the store to her house directly across Main Street.

It is not known if John Lane was partial to cigars, but it is believed that this gentleman spirit is Mr. Lane. Guests have come into the store asking if he is one of the street characters, and on a few occasions, others have mentioned how he simply vanished as they approached him. If this is indeed John, he seems to just want to watch the world rather than interact with it.

Employees also said that items have a tendency to move around in the store. Simple things, like candy that was placed on the front counter, has been found moved to the back shelf, where customers can't see the item; other times, it is placed in a perfectly straight line along the countertop. Shirts, along with other pieces of clothing, have been removed from hangers and draped willy-nilly over the racks when, just moments before, they had been neatly arranged. Employees even reported hearing strange tapping on the different signs around the store. Footsteps have been heard in the shop late at night by rangers patrolling the town, and store clerks have heard footsteps on the roof during Calico's Halloween Haunts event. The footsteps at night may, of course, be John Lane keeping watch over his goods, but why there would be footsteps on the roof is anybody's guess.

CALICO PHOTO STUDIO

Calico Photo Studio is your typical old-time photograph studio, where visitors go inside, don Wild West costumes, pick their pose and become instant cowboys and saloon girls. The difference here is, one shouldn't be surprised if there is an extra character in the picture when they get their photograph back.

According to Bill Cook, in his book *Ghostly Guide to Calico Ghost Town*, there is a spirit in the photo shop that they have named Joe. Joe likes to play around by causing prop bottles to fall over on the bar and roll just to the edge before suddenly stopping and falling to the floor. Bill said that this has happened so often that they managed to catch it on a television news show that was filming a segment about Calico's ghost walk. A current employee of the shop said that, even though the bottles have been moved to a higher shelf, they still have a tendency to fall over, roll to the edge and stop precariously before they fall. It seems that, even though Bill and his wife have moved on, Joe hasn't.

Another thing that Joe seems to enjoy is causing all of the framed photos of men to fall face-down, while he allows all of the frames with women in them to remain safely upright. Bill also mentions this in his book, and this story was confirmed by a current employee. Joe must fancy himself a ladies' man who doesn't want to look at the pictures of men. So, if you happen to get a nice character photograph of you and your partner or family and you find a strange cowboy looking back from the picture, don't worry, it's just Joe giving you something to remember him by.

CALICO PRINT SHOP

This store was originally the home of the *Calico Print* newspaper. Today, it serves as a bookstore and souvenir shop that sells cards, shot glasses and a number of fine tourist wares. It also seems to be the home of at least one cowboy. This cowboy has been seen by a few children but has been heard by both kids and adults. Kayla, the manager at the print shop, said that there was a young boy who was standing near a postcard stand when one of the cards lifted out of the rack, moved forward and fell at the boy's feet. The boy looked a bit pale after this happened, but he picked up the card and began smiling when he looked at it. He went and showed his family members, who were standing next to Kayla at the time, what was on the card. When they

This postcard carrousel in the Calico Print Shop is where the cowboy "gave" a postcard to a young boy.

looked at the postcard, the picture on it was that of a cowboy. The child grinned at them, pointed at the back-right corner of the store and said, "It was the cowboy right there who gave me the picture." The back-right corner is where the ghost of a cowboy is most frequently seen and heard.

Kayla also said that this spirit will make the employees sick to their stomachs. She, unfortunately, was a victim of this phenomenon one day. She told us that she had come into work feeling fine, but only a few minutes after opening the store, she began to feel nauseous and drained. This went on all day until she felt someone yank the back of her hair, pulling her head up to face the back-right corner. This happened at the same time that the postcard flew off the rack and landed at the boy's feet. This act of making the employees sick may be why some have said the cowboy is "not a very nice spirit." It seems that, if he does have a nasty side, it is not extended to children.

Next to Calico Print Shop are the remains of Joe's Saloon. This building burned down and was never rebuilt. There is a legend about a gambler who was a cheat and was caught in the act at Joe's. One of the gamblers he

All that remains of Joe's Saloon.

cheated shot the man, but the con artist managed to get out of the saloon and stumble down into Wall Street Canyon behind the bar. When the other patrons in Joe's came out to finish the man off, he was gone, and only a trace of blood and a few hoof prints were found to show where he had landed. The cheat managed to get away with a small fortune in gold and silver from those he had swindled.

A few days after he escaped Calico, the charlatan tried his antics in Las Vegas. Those he was gambling with in Sin City quickly caught on, and this time, when the bullets rang out, they found their mark. It is said that the last thing the man said before he died was, "The gold and silver bag…it's still at Calico." People still look for this bag of treasure today. The tales about the size of the ore bag have grown over the years, but that could just be because the ore is now worth much more than it was in the 1800s. Still, there are those who continue to search Wall Street Canyon and the surrounding hills, hoping to find the buried treasure and strike it rich.

R&D Fossils and Minerals

This shop near the center of town was, at one point, the Calico Theater. It now serves, as its name implies, as a place where visitors can buy crystals, minerals, healing stones and even petrified wood. In the second area of the large store, guests can find fine jewelry, commemorative magnets of all shapes and sizes and keepsakes for the whole family. Visitors to this store can also find a ghost who loves to play pranks and who is very protective of his employees.

The employees of this shop have said that the ghost is sort of a practical joker. One day, while counting the money drawer at the end of the day, one of the clerks heard what sounded like the marble bowl tipping over. Sure enough, as she stood there watching, a line of marbles came rolling across the floor. The odd thing was that, even though the floor was slightly slanted down from the direction the marbles had rolled, they stopped directly in front of her instead of continuing to roll past like they should have. In fact, since the marble bowl was so far away, not only should they have continued rolling, they should have gained enough speed to have sped past her. This has happened a few times since, but it is not always all of the marbles that roll down. Sometimes, it is a few, and other times, it might be only one marble—it just depends on the ghost's mood.

There is a statuette of a Native American on a high shelf behind the cash register in the lower store. This metal figure is supposed to be facing the front so that guests and customers can see it clearly. There have been many times that, while opening the store, the statue has been found facing a different direction. This phenomenon has even occurred during the day, when the store is busy. Employees will look up, see that the figure has been moved, turn it back and then find it facing a different way just minutes or hours later. On occasion, a handprint will appear on the statuette, which is sometimes hard to remove. Today, the employees mostly leave the print in place instead of continuously trying to remove it.

The ghost is also a music critic. The tuner for the shop is in the manager's office, usually behind a locked door. There have been times when a certain type of music has been playing and the station has mysteriously switched to a country western music channel. The spirit loves Johnny Cash and positively hates Elvis Presley. Whenever Elvis is heard over the radio, it is almost immediately switched to a Johnny Cash song or, if Cash isn't available, will simply turn off. On other occasions, the radio will simply turn off if the music is not what the spirit is in the mood for.

The store was once closed for a few weeks for renovation, and when the employees opened back up after the renovation was completed, they found the store in complete disarray. Shot glasses had been broken, merchandise had been tossed from the shelves and other items had been thrown across the store from display stands. As this is not typical behavior for the spirit, the employees could only guess that the ghost was upset about being alone for so long. After the renovation, a new alarm was installed that needed an employee to set it at the end of each workday. The alarm box has two lights that show its condition: red for when the alarm is off and green for when the alarm is set. There are times when the clerks are trying to leave for the day but are unable to get the alarm to turn on. No matter how hard they try, they simply cannot get it to set. They have discovered that if they tell the spirit they need to go home and ask him nicely to set the alarm, it will go from red to green almost immediately.

The spirit also doesn't like it when the clerks don't tidy up the store or do the required end-of-day walkthrough. If they have failed in this task, the keys that are needed to lock up for the night will not be where the clerks had left them. When this happens, the first place the clerks check is next to the cash register, on the counter. If they find them there, they know that the ghost is reminding them to tidy up and do the walkthrough. The spirit will, on occasion, play with the girls who work in the store. They have said that they

John King himself is believed to be watching over this souvenir store.

sometimes feel their hair being stroked and their backs being rubbed, and one clerk said she even had her pigtails tugged on.

There is a rocking chair in the storage area of the upper section of the store that will, on occasion, begin rocking for no reason. When this has happened, a few of the clerks have gone back to see what might be causing the chair to move, but as they neared the storage room, the door suddenly closed. It may be that the spirit doesn't want to be disturbed while he relaxes. The ghost also likes to be informed of any new inventory that comes in before it is placed out for sale. A few times, after new items have been put out on the sales floor, the employees will come in to find those items in complete disarray. Once, after a shipment of decorative treasure chests had been set out, the clerks found that they had been moved all over both stores and in places that were hard to reach. The clerks began to notice that this only happened to new items, so they began to tell the spirit when a shipment was arriving and what it was they would be selling. The movement of these wares stopped after he was told about the new arrivals.

The spirit seems to be protective of the girls who work in the store, which was made clear when the manager's son came in to help arrange things after the renovation was complete. Her son had never been in the shop before, and while he was removing some items from a shelf to another display, he was joking with his mother in a playfully aggressive way. The manager began to hear the familiar sound of the spirit's boots walking across the floor, but they were louder and faster than normal, and they were headed toward her son. She realized that the sound of the boots carried an angry walking tone, so she quickly called out to the spirit that the man was her son and that he was just playing around with her. The footsteps stopped immediately and were heard walking back across the store, away from her son.

The employees believe that the spirit that watches after them and their store is none other than John King himself. They believe this because the ghost has been seen by the clerks. A dark figure has been seen standing next to the storage room door, and every once in a while, they will see a man watching them and the store from the corner of their eye; of course, when they turn to look, the figure is gone. In one remarkable instance, the manager and another employee clearly saw a very tall, broad-shouldered figure in western clothing standing between the two stores. They said that the man looked just like the picture of John King they had seen many times. Another reason the clerks may believe that this apparition is the man who started the Silver King Mine is that his head—only his head—has been seen many times, walking from the Fossil Shop to the Calico Jail directly next door. This head wears the same type of hat that was favored by King, and since he was a lawman that watched over Calico, it makes sense that he would spend time at the jail. The theory of why we only see King's head has to do with the fact that, when King was alive, the Fossil Shop building was closer to ground level. Not knowing how time and perception work in the spirit world, we have to assume that King is walking where he is familiar, but since we see the new structure, we can only see his head as he walks.

There is another spirit that is seen both inside and outside the fossil shop. Before Calico was burned and left for dead, the Calico Theater stood where the lower store now sits. Sometime in the 1800s, an actress was on stage and, somehow, inadvertently fell off the rise, broke her neck and died. The actress was wearing a white formal dress (à la the Swedish Nightingale, Jenny Lind) and a big, frilly white hat when she died, making her very easy to spot today. This poor young lady has been seen standing on the landing directly in front of the fossil shop doors on many occasions. However, she is seen more often inside the Fossil Shop.

The actress likes to make herself known by appearing in the glass display cases while they are being cleaned. It doesn't matter if its day or night; there have been many times that a crew has been wiping down the glass, only to

You can just make out a handprint on this statuette that one of the ghosts in the Fossil and Mineral Shop likes to turn.

see a woman wearing a white dress and giant hat staring back at them. The workers quickly turn around to look, but of course, find no one there. When they turn back, the image is usually gone, but there have been times that the lady remained. Everyone who has seen this vision has said that the woman has a sad look on her face. This spirit is only seen in the lower store and could possibly be the reason the drawer on the old cash register is unable to remain closed every now and then.

Even guests have felt the presence of the ghosts at the fossil shop. We were informed there have been many times that customers have told the clerks about a sudden cold that comes upon them; they said that they had heard the phantom boot falls and whispers, and they even said that they were lightly touched—this last is only experienced by women. The R&D Fossil and Minerals Store may be the most haunted shop in Calico today.

Basket and Candle Shop and the Old Bathhouse

This building, it is said, was the original bathhouse for those in Calico who wanted to keep clean. According to Bill Cook, it was also used as a maintenance shed by Walter Knott during the town's restoration. Today, it is the Basket and Candle Shop; there, guests can find baskets for any type of use, as well as scented candles, incense and other items to make their homes smell like an English garden or a Christmas cinnamon wonderland. Guests can also create their own colorful candles for a small price; they might even get some help from the resident ghost.

Kayla, manager of the Calico Print Shop, said that, while she was working in the Candle Shop, the parasols they have on display, which hang from the ceiling, began to spin. According to her, there was no wind to speak of—no fan blowing in the shop nor any other discernable reason for the parasols to be moving, let alone spinning. If this wasn't strange enough, Kayla said that the parasols were spinning in different directions. One parasol was spinning clockwise, while the other, which was right next to it, was spinning counterclockwise. Each parasol spun in its own direction, with no rhyme or reason for which direction each was turning.

The spirit here seems to be a female and has been seen by both guests and employees. One employee said that she was once alone in the shop when she clearly heard her name called. The voice was that of a woman and was spoken directly next to where she was standing by the register. Another clerk

The Basket and Candle Shop seems to have at least one spirit that seems to be jealous of the female employees.

said that it seemed like the spirit made her sick after talking to a handsome customer; again, her name was softly called as she was talking, and right afterward, she became violently ill. The clerk believes that the spirit may have a jealous streak in her. On another occasion, the employee heard what sounded like a camera taking a picture. This happened twice, even though there was no one in the store or out on the porch. When the clerk went to see who or what made the sounds, a porcelain doll flew off one of the shelves and smashed face-down on the floor, breaking apart in the process.

The back storeroom is another area where some of the employees don't like to go. Boot falls are sometimes heard there, especially when someone is using the restroom, which is in the storeroom area. Oftentimes, while employees are using the restroom, they will hear someone walking around, things being moved about, whispered voices and someone coming up to the closed bathroom door. Many of the female employees refuse to use the restroom and will go across the street to the Calico Print Shop instead. The spirit never seems to bother the guests who come into the shop, but many have told the clerks that they heard whispers and felt cold spots, and they have asked about the footsteps they hear in the backroom.

MISCELLANEOUS MISCHIEF

There is one other location that the spirits of Calico like to haunt. The first time we heard about it was on the town ghost walk, and to be perfectly honest, we thought it was a parting joke told to amuse us guests and to also let us know where the bathroom was located if we needed to use the facilities. After more research on the town, we found that our guides were actually telling us another ghost story—albeit, in an entertaining and amusing way.

It seems that the women's bathroom to the right of Main Street, just past the Leather Shop, is haunted. The tour guides told the group of us that women who use the restroom will hear the voices of other females, even though they know no one else is there. The guides then went on to say that a black smoke is often seen wafting up from the building and that it oftentimes moves away, down the street. One can see why we assumed the guides were just making fun of a restroom.

Calico also has numerous reports of ghostly figures moving about town during the day, but they are mostly seen in the evening and at night. Dorsey, the mail-carrying dog is also seen in Calico, usually near the Calico Print Shop, where the old post office used to be. At the ruins of the old China

The Calico Cemetery has known its share of hardships. Perhaps this is why so many spirits walk its hallowed ground.

Town area, voices are sometimes heard speaking Chinese, and ghostly lights and orbs are commonplace. There are also rare reports of sightings from the town jail and barber shop. The Calico Cemetery, with its lost graves and missing names, has its share of activity as well. From a black shadow figure that simply appears from the left side and walks between the two small graves of the Cochran children to the spirit that is believed to be that of fourteen-year-old Bobby Stephens, who was buried there before Calico was even a town, the cemetery is notably haunted. Planet Paranormal team members even managed to catch an EVP (electronic voice phenomenon) on one of their night investigations; they caught a man telling them to "f— off" when they asked about being buried in the hard desert earth.

Calico, the epitome of the pioneering spirit.

EPILOGUE

When we began writing this book, our biggest concern was whether we had enough information on this small historic town to be able to fill a whole book. As we researched, we began to realize that we may not have enough room to be able to get across just how important Calico is to the history of California and the Mojave Desert. We also needed to tell the large number of ghost tales that came from the employees who work at the town today, along with those that have been reported over the many years since Calico was founded.

We tried to make this work both a comprehensive history of Calico and a true representation of the spirits who still call the town home—and who, it seems, have called Calico home since its early days. We hope we have succeeded and that you have both learned from and enjoyed what you have read.

For those of you who want to go and experience the town for yourself, we can't stress strongly enough that you should, by all means, go and marvel at this town in the desert. For those of you who want to know more about the ghostly activity, we highly recommend taking one of the fantastic ghost walks the town offers. Because even though we referenced a sampling of the ghost stories we learned from these walks, nothing beats being on one of those tours and learning from those who are there every day, seeing and experiencing the haunts of Calico. You may also experience the haunts for yourself while on a ghost walk. It's something you don't want to miss.

To put it simply: Yes, Virginia, there are ghosts in Calico!

BIBLIOGRAPHY

Books

Cook, Bill. *Ghostly Guide to Calico Ghost Town*. Long Beach, CA: Magic Valley Publishers, 2008.

Lane, Lucy Bell. *Calico Memories*. Barstow, CA: Mojave River Valley Museum, 1993.

Payton, Paige M. *Calico*. Charleston, SC: Arcadia Publishing, 2012.

Websites

California Digital Newspaper Collection. "*Santa Cruz Sentinel*, Volume 100, Number 44, 21 February 1955." Center for Biographical Studies and Research. www.cdnc.ucr.edu.

Core, Tom. "Bearly Remembered." www.bigbeargrizzly.net.

Daggett Museum. "Daggett Historical Brief." www.mojavedesert.net.

Gold, Scott. "Fire Destroys Part of Calico Ghost Town. *Los Angeles Times*, July 25, 2001. www.latimes.com.

Iffrig, Kurt. "Calico Mines." Lost Mines of Southern California. www.secretmines.com.

Kelly, Kate. "A Dog Who Delivered the Mail." America Comes Alive! www.americacomesalive.com.

Knox, Thomas Wallace. "Dorsey the Mail Dog." Old-Time Farm Shepherd. www.oldtimefarmshepherd.org.

LeBlanc, Jocelyne. "10 Interesting Facts About the Tommyknocker Legend." TopTenz. www.toptenz.net.

McIntyre, Emmett. "The Faeries of the Cornish Tin Mines—Cousin Jack and the TommyKnockers." Transceltic. www.transceltic.com.

Mojo on the Mojave. "Siblings of SoCal, Calico Ghost Town and Knott's Berry Farm." Desert USA. www.desertusa.com.

Rockwell, Rick. "The Grave Mysteries of Calico's Historic Cemetery." CalEXPLORnia. www.calexplornia.com.

Smith, Peggy. "Calico Cemetery." U.S. Cemetery Project. www.uscemeteryproj.com.

Travel Geek, The. "Calico Cemetery—Clues About the Mining Community." www.wend.ca.

Vasconcellos, Ramon. "Ghost Town: Calico, California." www.historynet.com.

ABOUT THE AUTHORS

BRIAN CLUNE IS THE cofounder and historian for Planet Paranormal Radio and Planet Paranormal Investigations. He has traveled around the entire state of California, researching its haunted hot spots and historical locations in an effort to bring knowledge of the paranormal and the wonderful history of the state to those who are interested in learning.

His interest in history has led him to volunteer aboard the USS *Iowa* and at the Fort MacArthur Military Museum and to give lectures at colleges and universities around the state. He has been involved with numerous television shows, including *Ghost Adventures*, *My Ghost Story*, *Dead Files* and *Ghost Hunters*, and he was the subject in a companion documentary for the movie *Paranormal Asylum*. He has also appeared on numerous local, national and international radio programs.

His other books include *California's Historic Haunts* (published by Schiffer Books), the highly acclaimed *Ghosts of the Queen Mary* (published by The History Press) and *Ghosts and Legends of Alcatraz*, along with *Haunted Universal Studios* (published by The History Press), all with coauthor Bob Davis. Brian and Bob also teamed up to write the riveting biography of ghost box creator, Frank Sumption. Brian is also the author of *Haunted San Pedro and Hollywood Obscura*, the spellbinding book that deals with Hollywood's dark and sordid tales of murder and ghosts. He is currently working on books about the haunts of San Diego, California, the legends and lore of California's Highway 395 and the cryptids of California; he is working on the last book with his son Carmel.

Clune lives in Southern California with his loving wife, Terri, his three wonderful children and, of course, Wandering Wyatt! Watch for Wyatt as you read this book and others we have written.

BOB DAVIS IS A commercial real estate investor by day and a paranormal researcher by night. Bob co-owns Planet Paranormal Radio, Planet Paranormal Investigations and Queen Mary Shadows along with Ash Blackwell and Brian Clune. Bob lives in Southern California with his lovely wife, Miyu, and his son, Nick. His daughter, Katrina, who is also a paranormal researcher, is currently living and investigating in Arizona, where Planet Paranormal investigators enjoy investigating new locations.

Mr. Davis has been featured on over thirty-five radio broadcasts nationally and internationally, ten books and publications and two documentary films. In addition, he has been published in the *New York Daily News*, *World News*, the *Los Angeles Examiner* and the *Paranormal Examiner* and has been seen on such hit television shows as *Ghost Hunters*, *Ghost Adventures*, *My Ghost Story* and *The Dead Files*.

THE AUTHORS OF THIS book also authored *Ghosts of the Queen Mary*, which was featured in the October 2015 edition of *LIFE Magazine*'s "World's Most Haunted," as the subject matter for the Queen Mary article. It is now part of *LIFE*'s Classic series and is rereleased annually.

Planet Paranormal's
Guide to the Other Side